STUDIES IN AMERICAN POPULAR HISTORY AND CULTURE

Edited by

Jerome Nadelhaft
University of Maine

A ROUTLEDGE SERIES

STUDIES IN AMERICAN POPULAR HISTORY AND CULTURE

JEROME NADELHAFT, *General Editor*

THE MAKING OF THE PRIMITIVE BAPTISTS
A Cultural and Intellectual History of the Antimission Movement, 1800–1840
James R. Mathis

WOMEN AND COMEDY IN SOLO PERFORMANCE
Phyllis Diller, Lily Tomlin, and Roseanne
Suzanne Lavin

THE LITERATURE OF IMMIGRATION AND RACIAL FORMATION
Becoming White, Becoming Other, Becoming American in the Late Progressive Era
Linda Joyce Brown

POPULAR CULTURE AND THE ENDURING MYTH OF CHICAGO, 1871–1968
Lisa Krissoff Boehm

AMERICA'S FIGHT OVER WATER
The Environmental and Political Effects of Large-Scale Water Systems
Kevin Wehr

DAUGHTERS OF EVE
Pregnant Brides and Unwed Mothers in Seventeenth-Century Massachusetts
Else L. Hambleton

NARRATIVE, POLITICAL UNCONSCIOUS, AND RACIAL VIOLENCE IN WILMINGTON, NORTH CAROLINA
Leslie H. Hossfeld

VALIDATING BACHELORHOOD
Audience, Patriarchy, and Charles Brockden Brown's Editorship of the Monthly Magazine and American Review
Scott Slawinski

CHILDREN AND THE CRIMINAL LAW IN CONNECTICUT, 1635–1855
Changing Perceptions of Childhood
Nancy Hathaway Steenburg

BOOKS AND LIBRARIES IN AMERICAN SOCIETY DURING WORLD WAR II
Weapons in the War of Ideas
Patti Clayton Becker

MISTRESSES OF THE TRANSIENT HEARTH
American Army Officers' Wives and Material Culture, 1840–1880
Robin Dell Campbell

THE FARM PRESS, REFORM, AND RURAL CHANGE, 1895–1920
John J. Fry

STATE OF 'THE UNION'
Marriage and Free Love in the Late 1800s
Sandra Ellen Schroer

"MY PEN AND MY SOUL HAVE EVER GONE TOGETHER"
Thomas Paine and the American Revolution
Vikki J. Vickers

AGENTS OF WRATH, SOWERS OF DISCORD
Authority and Dissent in Puritan Massachusetts, 1630–1655
Timothy L. Wood

THE QUIET REVOLUTIONARIES
How the Grey Nuns Changed the Social Welfare Paradigm of Lewiston, Maine
Susan P. Hudson

THE QUIET REVOLUTIONARIES
How the Grey Nuns Changed the Social Welfare Paradigm of Lewiston, Maine

Susan P. Hudson

Routledge
Taylor & Francis Group

NEW YORK AND LONDON

Published in 2006 by
Routledge
Taylor & Francis Group
711 Third Avenue
New York, NY 10017

Published in Great Britain by
Routledge
Taylor & Francis Group
2 Park Square
Milton Park, Abingdon
Oxon OX14 4RN

Routledge is an imprint of Taylor & Francis Group

First issued in paperback 2012

International Standard Book Number-13: 978-0-415-97834-7 (Hardcover)
International Standard Book Number-13: 978-0-415-65125-7 (Paperback)
Library of Congress Card Number 2005035748

Library of Congress Cataloging-in-Publication Data

Hudson, Susan Pearman.
   The quiet revolutionaries : how the Grey Nuns changed the social welfare paradigm of Lewiston, Maine / Susan P. Hudson.
      p. cm. -- (Studies in American popular history and culture)
   Includes bibliographical references and index.
   ISBN 0-415-97834-3
   1. Soeurs grises--Maine--Lewiston--History--19th century. 2. Nuns--Maine--Lewiston--History--19th century. 3. Lewiston (Me.)--History--19th century. I. Title. II. Series: American popular history and culture (Routledge (Firm))

BX4366.Z5M3 2006
271'.91074182--dc22   2005035748

Taylor & Francis Group
is the Academic Division of Informa plc.

Visit the Taylor & Francis Web site at
http://www.taylorandfrancis.com

and the Routledge Web site at
http://www.routledge-ny.com

To
Steven A. Hudson, for being a real husband
and Sister Jacqueline Peloquin, SOC, for being a real friend

Contents

List of Figures[1]

Acknowledgments

This book represents years of research and writing. I have been sustained and encouraged by the Grey Nuns of Saint-Hyacinthe, Quebec. I thank in particular the former Portland Superior of the Sisters of Charity, Jacqueline Peloquin, who read the manuscript with careful attention while providing the unique insight of a woman religious. Her contribution helped me to avoid pitfalls common to histories on congregations of women religious and maintain historical criticism.

Over the years, I have attended conferences and given numerous papers and talks informed by my research for this book. Members of Maine's academic community have welcomed my scholarship while providing both opportunities and constructive commentary. I am indebted to Billie Gammon, Jerry Nadelhaft, Douglas Hodgkin and Bates College Library.

Gary Gerstle and Larry Poos gave invaluable support and intellectual vigor in the formative period of this book. Their confidence in my work and their perspective on the challenges associated with my writing gave me the courage to continue. Without their involvement this book may never have begun, or much less been completed.

Numerous friendships have formed during the years. Several members of the Catholic clergy of the Portland See have welcomed my work and opened their parish records for my research. Rick Spear, director of the Lewiston Public Library, has given a tremendous amount of support while being a valuable source of local information. Nick Creary faithfully maintained my connection with my colleagues as I wrote in the isolation of Maine's hinterland. My deepest thanks belong to my family; those who have been with me from the earliest days of my research and those who were born during it. Their love has strengthened me during the trying periods of this work and their aptitude for the world of computers has made it possible for me to finish.

The Daughters of Madame d'Youville

Marguerite d'Youville was born Marie-Marguerite Du Frost de Lajem-merais at Varennes, in Quebec on October 15, 1701. Her family could rightfully claim minor French nobility, but due to the death of her father in 1708 the family lacked economic stability. In 1737, six years after the death of her husband and four of her six children, Marguerite founded the Congregation des Soeurs de la Charité or "Soeurs Grises," commonly known as the Grey Nuns. The order received patent Letters of Approval from King Louis XV in 1753. Marguerite d'Youville died on December 23, 1771. Pope John XXIII named her the Mother of Universal Charity and she was canonized on November 9, 1990 by Pope John Paul II who bestowed upon her the title of "Model of Compassion." Marguerite d'Youville is the first Canadian-born Roman Catholic saint.[1]

The harsh realities that defined Marguerite d'Youville's life evolved into the stimuli that compelled her and her order into the world of hospital care from Montreal, Quebec to Lewiston, Maine. This drive was augmented by her professional achievements as a successful merchant and tradeswoman. In the words of Rachel Naomi Remen, Marguerite had learned to "harvest [her] failures."[2] During her lifetime Marguerite had suffered abuse, abandonment, poverty, family tragedy, death, and the British conquest of her people and nation yet she did not turn to anger, but rather chose to find comfort in a spirituality that was grounded on a devotion to a Providential God. The death of her father in childhood, followed by a young widowhood, nurtured Marguerite's spirituality to a male God that was omnipotent and always present. The strength of her devotion gave her personal power which directed her outwardly away from a traditional convent life as a woman religious. Using the resources of the Catholic structures of her Quebecois society, Marguerite mitigated poverty and illness by assuming the authority to administer Montreal's Hospital General in 1747.

Marguerite, while an eighteenth-century widow, was nevertheless emerging as a powerful activist. Her participation in hospital care began a social movement that eventually spread to Lewiston. Marguerite's acquisition of the cultural and religious power necessary for her successful administration of the Hospital General gave her permanence in a structured resource recognized by the civic community. The legacy of Marguerite d'Youville became the heritage of the Grey Nuns of Saint-Hyacinthe and was passed down faithfully from sister to novice to postulant.

A Sister of Charity of Saint-Hyacinthe, Grey Nuns, received her spiritual formation under the direct supervision of the order's novice mistress, and the general authority of all the professed sisters at the Grey Nuns' motherhouse in Saint-Hyacinthe, Quebec. During the nineteenth century, the normal age that a young woman made her profession as a Grey Nun was between eighteen and twenty-five.[3] Of the seventy professed Grey Nuns who worked in Lewiston, from 1878 to 1908, seventeen made their profession before they were twenty, four made their profession in their earlier thirties and the rest were all in their twenties.

When a young woman asked admittance into the Grey Nuns' order there was first a short trial period when she was a postulant, after which she was either accepted into the community or asked to leave. A Grey Nun postulant received a modified Grey Nun habit indicating her status within the community as a novice. During the formative decades of the Saint-Hyacinthe community 1840–1890, permanent vows were professed after a two-year trial period.

Upon making her permanent vows, the novice exchanged her habit for the black bonnet and the taupe habit of a professed Grey Nun. When a Grey Nun worked as a nurse within a hospital environment she usually substituted her taupe habit for a white habit. Spiritually joined to the Christian virtue of charity, a Grey Nun novice professed the three standard vows of a Catholic religious: chastity, obedience, and poverty. As a member of the Grey Nun order, however, she also made a fourth vow of service to the poor. It was commonly acknowledged in congregations of sister-nurses that a life of service was based upon their "underlying religious and theological" self-understanding.[4] The Grey Nuns took the additional step of formalizing this mission in their fourth vow, and thus sanctified it. According to Canon Law, these vows are termed "simple" due to the fact that the Grey Nuns are an active community and thereby not confined to a cloister. "Solemn" vows are professed by women religious who spend their lives enclosed in a cloister, such as the congregations of Poor Claire or the Carmelites.

In addition to professing her religious vows, a Grey Nun would promise to live according to the rules of the community's constitution. Both of these conditions are clearly stated in the community's *Constitutions and Rules, Of the Congregation of the Sisters of Charity of Saint-Hyacinthe,* which was first composed in 1840:

> "The Form of vows.
>
> To arrive at perfect charity with the grace of the Holy Spirit and the aid of the Virgin Mary, before the persons here assembled, into your hands, I make the vows of chastity, of poverty, and obedience in service to the poor, according to the constitutions and rules of the Sisters of Charity of Saint-Hyacinthe."[5]

The professing of temporary vows by the order was not instituted until 1891. From that time, temporary vows were taken two years after becoming a novice with permanent vows professed five years later. There were exceptions made to this rule. If the novice's skills were needed and the community believed her to be ready to make her final profession prior to fulfilling the five-year time requirement she was professed. When a young woman professed her permanent vows as a Grey Nun, they represented a total commitment by her to the community and to the Catholic Church for the duration of her natural life. An extremely few professed Grey Nuns did leave the community and return to secular life. It was a statistically insignificant number of women whose reason and/or motivation remained private.

It was during her years as a novice that a Grey Nun was spiritually formed and subsumed into the particular religious culture which was practiced by the Grey Nuns. To avoid singularity, a Grey Nun novice usually conformed to the will of the community. A Grey Nun's definition of self, and her individual relationship to her religious community, was not, however one of elusiveness. Rather, a Grey Nun's understanding of self was actually communal. A woman as a Grey Nun interiorized her religious community and bonded her own self-identity to the communal identity of the order. "She was never alone because there was no alone."[6] While this may seem in our contemporary society to have required an inordinate forfeit of individuality to the collective identity of the order it was nevertheless, also, the time when a novice began an individualized and professional education in health care and social work. Through a training process of inter-community mentoring and internship at the Hôtel-Dieu, the novice was exposed to medical knowledge and professional opportunities that would have been denied her if she was not a sister-nurse. For thousands of Catholic women, prior to the last decades of the twentieth century, religious identity was the avenue which allowed them "to present and assert

themselves in private and public ways." It was an avenue to achievement
that "enabled them to rely on an authority beyond the world of men and
provided crucial support for those who stepped beyond accepted bonds."[7]

The Grey Nuns had established the Hôtel-Dieu to provide hospital
care after four members of the Sisters of Charity of Montreal, Grey Nuns,
founded the Saint-Hyacinthe community in 1840. The history of the founding of the Hôtel-Dieu and the Saint-Hyacinthe community with its poverty,
epidemics, and social dislocation, illustrates the enormous challenge that
the Grey Nuns accepted as women religious. A similar challenge would
again be accepted when they established their community and hospital in
Lewiston.

On May 4, 1840 four Grey Nuns of Montreal with the support and
blessing of their community and the aid of the Montreal's Bishop Ignace
Bourget, traveled by boat and wagon to establish a community in Saint-
Hyacinthe, Quebec. The sisters' names and ages were: Marie-Michel
Archange Thuot, fifty-three years old and the first Superior General of the
Saint-Hyacinthe community; Marie Tharsille Guyon, thirty-one years old;
Marie Honorine Pinsonnault, twenty-nine years old; and Marie-Emile Jauron, the youngest member of the group at twenty-four. Pinsonnault would
succeed Mother Thuot as the Saint-Hyacinthe Superior General in 1845
but would return to the Grey Nun community in Montreal in 1854. Jauron
followed Pinsonnault as the Superior of Saint-Hyacinthe from 1854 to
1865. Guyon would also leave the Saint-Hyacinthe community and return
to the Montreal community of Grey Nuns in 1854.

The journey from Montreal to the rural farming town of Saint-
Hyacinthe took three exhausting days. Once the sisters arrived at Saint-
Hyacinthe they immediately began a health care ministry for the diseased
and dependent of the city. Within four days of their arrival from Montreal
this tiny band established the Hôtel-Dieu to aid their ministry and adopted
the Montreal Grey Nuns' bylaws with minor modifications for their Saint-
Hyacinthe community. An English translation of two bylaws follows:

> "For these reasons, the Holy Name of God is invoked. We state and
> ordain the following.
>
> l-We establish and erect, with the present ordinance, Congregation of
> secular daughters under the title of Daughters of Charity, to administer
> a Hospital (Hôtel-Dieu) in the parish of Saint-Hyacinthe, and we give
> them permission to live in community while making the simple vows of
> poverty, chastity and obedience, 'and to serve the poor,' according to
> the rules and constitutions above mentioned.

Thus is the generous woman who, on May 8, 1840, with her three companions inaugurated in Saint-Hyacinthe 'Ministry of Tenderness' with the most diverse manifestation: Care of the poor and of the aged persons in the hospital, welcoming and educate orphans, visiting the poor and sick in their homes. To assure themselves of revenue permitting the help for the greatest number in need, the sisters will admit into their home several lady pensionnaires."[8]

The bylaws received final pontifical and diocesan approval fifty-six year later on July 10, 1896, and thus the Sisters of Charity of Saint-Hyacinthe, the Grey Nuns, became a separate pontifical branch of the Sisters of Charity of Montreal, the Grey Nuns. The Grey Nuns' constitution has been modified since 1896 in response to the order's growth and involvement in the world of modernity. Nevertheless, the Grey Nuns' principal mission as "servants of the poor in the Church as followers of Christ Jesus for the glory of God the Father" underlined the order's identity, governance, and spirituality and has remained consistent throughout the years.[9]

The Hôtel-Dieu in Saint-Hyacinthe would eventually expand into the city's largest hospital. In 1840 it was a drafty house, lacking insulation and built of green wood with little furniture and no winter provisions. The Hôtel-Dieu lacked even minimal standards of sanitation and comfort. According to the Grey Nuns' chronicles, the first years of occupation represented a time of "great suffering" and deprivation for the community. The Grey Nuns existed in extreme poverty. The sisters drank either an herbal mixture of wild tea which they called "wood tea" or a concoction of cereals and barley mixed into a coffee paste they simply named "barley coffee." Breakfast for the community, when available, consisted of cornbread and water. Any milk, butter, or sugar was always given to their patients.

The lack of sanitation at Hôtel-Dieu, coupled with the effects of malnutrition, cold and exhaustion, claimed the life of the first professed Grey Nun in the Saint-Hyacinthe community, Elizabeth Bovin. Sister Bovin died, presumably of cholera, at the age of twenty-three on November 22, 1843. Her early death reduced the community to four professed sisters and three in formation. Seven women now were faced with the challenge of providing the only formal health care between the cities of Montreal and Quebec. Despite the harsh conditions, the community in Saint-Hyacinthe survived and prospered. True to their religious self-understanding of being one with the poor and their unwillingness to accept the lack of social welfare services to the poor, the sisters became the region's health care providers to infants, the infirm, the diseased and the dependent.

As the Grey Nun community secured stability in Saint-Hyacinthe they initiated vocational and farming activities while also providing educational opportunities for the poor as industrialization transformed the region. The pace of industrialization for this farm community was such that by 1910, a map of Saint-Hyacinthe listed twenty industries such as: the Saint-Hyacinthe Distillery Company, Ltd.; the Vinegar Factory of Saint-Hyacinthe; D. Chalifourx & Sons, Limited, which was comprised of a mounting department, a forge, a machine shop, and a foundry; and, Augustin & Daudelin who were machinists and engineers. There were also three banks, two clubs and the Hotel Ottawa. The Grey Nuns participated in the beginning of this industrial transformation as another facet of their ministerial and entrepreneurial activities. On April 26, 1864 the Grey Nuns' established the workhouse of Sainte-Genevieve. The stated reason for the effort was: "[I]n the purpose of procuring work for the poor women when they are unable to find any [work] on the outside."[10] The Grey Nuns' enterprise was so successful that by 1871 their workhouse was producing woolen fabric and soap while providing employment for ten women, fifteen girls, one man and three boys.[11] The Grey Nuns' success continued at such a rate that by 1878, the business had exceeded the capacity of its original building. A new facility was required to meet the demand. The Grey Nuns immediately responded. Within two years the sisters had purchased additional real estate, built a new facility and opened an expanded workhouse on September 8, 1880.[12] Their aggressive and successful response to this situation was characteristic of the order and was repeatedly seen when the sisters confronted challenges when they ministered in Lewiston.

The separate establishment of a Grey Nun community in Saint-Hyacinthe and the success of the Sainte-Genevieve workhouse demonstrated that the Saint-Hyacinthe Grey Nuns had stabilized and expanded their community and social action ministry within the four decades prior to their acceptance of a mission to the United States in Lewiston, Maine. The Grey Nuns' achievement also paralleled the demographic and industrial expansion of the town of Saint-Hyacinthe which occurred during the second half of the nineteenth century. As a consequence, the Grey Nuns individually and collectively, were well aware of the ramifications caused by the transformation of a rural community to a "commercial and service center."[13]

The direct involvement of the Grey Nuns with alleviating the attendant poverty and disease as the city of Saint-Hyacinthe evolved gave the sisters an understanding of what was required to mitigate rural poverty and the potential social dislocation caused by industrialization. In the words of a Saint-Hyacinthe Grey Nun:

"The rural location of Saint-Hyacinthe supported an aspect of Saint Marguerite d'Youville that emphasized the sisters' closeness with poverty. It [Saint-Hyacinthe] was in 1840 a rural farming community that endured long isolating harsh winters. If the summer crops failed the consequences could be disastrous. So the spiritual virtue of charity, which we profess, was physically manifested in our natural environment. There was a willingness among the sisters to join their lives with the lives of the poor whom they served. We all worked together to survive. There was no distinction among us. Everyone was poor."[14]

Introduction

The women who comprised the nineteenth-century Lewiston, Maine community of the Sisters of Charity of Saint-Hyacinthe, Quebec (known as the Grey Nuns) were entrepreneurs, builders, sister-nurses, educators, trustees, administrators, chaplains, CEO's and CFO's. With their founding of the first hospital in Lewiston, the Asylum of our Lady of Lourdes in 1888, a healing ministry was born that continues to the present, today as Saint Mary's Regional Medical Center. This establishment was a significant event in the evolution of social welfare and medicine in Lewiston and the state of Maine.

Prior to the Grey Nuns' arrival, Lewiston's benevolent structures not only lacked an empathetic approach towards care but were dismissive of the severity of poverty, especially for French Canadian immigrants and the working poor. Through the establishment of the Asylum of Our Lady of Lourdes, the Hospital General Sainte-Marie, the Girls' Orphanage, and the Healy Asylum for Boys, the Grey Nuns founded a network of structured benevolent institutions that provided basic medical care, shelter and education to the lowest socioeconomic and immigrant classes.

The objective of the Grey Nuns' Lewiston hospitals was to mitigate physical suffering and mental anguish resulting from both physical and spiritual trauma. This foundation's goals mirrored those of the community's first hospital the Hôtel-Dieu in Saint-Hyacinthe, Quebec. Secularized medical care that characterizes contemporary hospital services was not the objective of these sister-nurses. One religious historian has argued that in fact "pastoral care" was the "principal force" in the ministry of the sister-nurse.[1] The sister-nurse achieved her objective of individualized care for her patient by utilizing a holistic approach that ministered to both the physical and spiritual needs of the patient. The primacy of professional physicians in our contemporary hospitals who only acknowledge a patient's physical aliments was not commonly recognized in pre-twentieth century hospitals. Rather sister-nurses believed that medical care was incomplete if it was limited to the physical manifestations of the illness.

This did not mean, however, that the sister-nurses were not eager to improve the quality of their medical knowledge. The Hôtel-Dieu evolved over the last decades of the nineteenth century from a health care facility that practiced a holistic attitude towards healing into a medical institution similar to an urban hospital. Structurally this transformation was guided by the organizational and managerial skills of the Grey Nuns. Both Patricia Wittberg and Sioban Nelson agree that the structures of a religious order not only "provid[ed] a career ladder rarely available to women elsewhere" but enabled resources to be expeditiously used. Sisters were trained during their spiritual formation to value submission and obedience to their religious superiors. This combination of providing intense training programs coupled with organizational obedience, allowed orders to effectively place skilled sisters in their institutions and expect success.[2] As seen by the dynamic expansion of the Grey Nun communities, this administrative guideline for the placement of human resources was astonishingly successful.

The Saint-Hyacinthe order of Grey Nuns established many communities in Quebec and the United States within sixty years of the founding of the order. Each community may have had one or more facilities under the authority of the motherhouse, such as schools, orphan asylums, welfare institutions, and hospitals. The following is a list of the various Saint-Hyacinthe Grey Nun communities and their dates of establishment: Sorel, Quebec on October 23, 1862; Marie Ville, Quebec on October 13, 1865; Hereford, Quebec on November 3, 1871; Sherbrooke, Quebec on April 21, 1875; Farnham, Quebec on May 4, 1876; Saint Johnsbury, Vermont on September 1877; Saint Denis-sur-Richelieu, Quebec on February 3, 1878; Lewiston, Maine on November 21, 1878; Holyoke, Massachusetts on October 8, 1881; Manchester, New Hampshire on December 9, 1885; and Berlin, New Hampshire on June 19, 1905.

The Grey Nuns and their institutions were collectively part of a vast network of women directed foundations that challenged the prevailing socio-cultural understanding of benevolent hospital and medical care. These women, though went further and deeper, and questioned the abilities and right, of male administrators, physicians, and priests to control Canadian and American medical and social welfare institutions. It was a battle for autonomy and control, which sister-nurses fought in habited obedience while independently forging structures that radically brought social service into urban America. The sisters, true to their humility, remained silent while bishops and physicians took the credit for their endeavors. This lack of recognition was not challenged by sister-nurses, for their goal was never public acclaim, but rather eternal salvation gained by living a selfless life in service to the suffering poor.

As will be explored in Chapters Three and Four, there was a significant socio-religious distinction between Catholic administered health care institutions and non-Catholic urban secular volunteer hospitals. The sister-nurses of Saint-Hyacinthe crafted their nursing to be an expression of their unique spirituality as the spiritual daughters of Saint Marguerite d'Youville. They did not interpret their care-giving skills as strictly belonging to the emerging professional community of secular nurses and hospital administrators. The act of care was a medium that transformed both patient and caregiver. The Grey Nuns marshaled their resources to transform the desperate needs of the poor into opportunities to establish a faith-based institutional health care network; first in Quebec and then in the United States. By building health care institutions, the sisters believed that they not only nursed the ill but that they "hastened the reign of God on earth" and brought salvation to the poor.[3] That these women also transformed the American hospital system was incidental to them. Unlike their secular counterparts, the Grey Nuns' primary objective was to mission to the poor as sister-nurses through acts of charity. It was this spirituality which was the powerful immeasurable asset of their institutions. Women religious individually and collectively drew their strength from this deep spirituality as they labored to build hospitals and social welfare structures throughout North, South and Central America.

There was no professional medical training at the Hôtel-Dieu until the twentieth century. During the early years, general medical knowledge and healing arts were passed from sister to novice as new sister-nurses were trained. As the decades passed, the nuns recognized the need to institute a more formalized medical training of individual sisters as they mastered the various disciplines of healing. In the Lewiston ministry the medical training that each Grey Nun brought with them is listed after individual sister's names in various archival records. To protect and honor the Grey Nuns' rules of confidentiality, this information is presented generally in the following work.[4]

According to archival records, as individual sisters acquired specific medical, and analytical and administrative skills, they were recognized professionally within the community by the Superior General and her Council. However, in institutional publications, such as hospital annual reports, there is never any recognition of the achievements of any individual Grey Nun. The Superior and/or her Council would assign the sister to one or several

occupations in their hospitals and care facilities according to her professional achievements, or their belief in her abilities, and the need of the institution in Lewiston. In Hospital General Sainte-Marie, the ministries
performed by a sister were determined by the department to which she was
assigned in accordance to her professional and medical abilities.[5]

The Superior of the community was the top administrator and super-
visor of the hospital and convent. Her responsibilities included the supervision of the religious and personal life of all the sisters in the community; the
general business management of the institutions; and administrative
responsibility over all the heads of the hospital's departments. The Superior
of the Lewiston community reported directly to the Superior General in
Saint-Hyacinthe and was responsible for any misconduct by the sisters or
lack of success in their ministry. The structure of both the religious community and the hospital was thus hierarchical and authoritarian, mirroring the
principles of nineteenth-century Catholicism. All the other sisters worked
underneath the Superior and their responsibilities varied. There were geriatric sister-nurses who were specialized caregivers and only took care of the
poor and sick elderly. A sister-nurse pharmacist was similarly specialized as
were technical assistants. The responsibilities of non-specialized sister-
nurses were broad and included ward supervision, nutrition, aiding secular
and student nurses, analytical, laboratory, x-ray facilities, and surgical
departments. Sister-nurses also provided child care for orphans, and the
children of working parents or the hospital residents. The non-medical
departments of the hospital and convent were similarly under the jurisdic-
tion of sisters who were trained in the field of secretarial work, domestic
responsibilities and liturgical practices. A sister who was assigned to the
business office was responsible for the hospital and convent finances, pur-
chasing and maintaining the storerooms.[6] There is no evidence to indicate
sister-nurses had access to either professional or medical training outside of
their institutions or were ever interned to a physician at Saint-Hyacinthe.
Of the surviving medical records written by the sister-nurses, they advised
the practice of a holistic approach towards disease that implemented a
regime of diet, rest and herbal remedies.

An accredited nursing school was not established at the Hôtel-Dieu
until 1902. The founding of this school correlates to the academic formal-
ization of nurse training programs which was occurring throughout the
North America. Lay physicians were invited into the nursing school to lec-
ture and train the sister-nurses in various medical procedures and care
methods. It is indicative of the practicality and desire for improving patient
care which characterized the Grey Nuns' leadership that they recognized
sister-nurses and their hospitals required the assistance of professionally

trained and educated nurses by the twentieth century. It is also consistent with their charism that the Grey Nuns did not look to secularly trained nurses to replace the sister-nurses in their institutions, but rather, educated the women within their community.

It was the Grey Nuns' religious self-understanding coupled with their professional training as sister-nurses which led to the transformation of structured benevolent care in late nineteenth-century Lewiston. Whether the Lewiston's Grey Nuns founded a hospital, an orphanage, a school or created a place of refuge for the destitute, the unwanted, and the terminally ill, their foundations became the physical expression of the congregation's social welfare aspirations. The contribution of the Grey Nuns, both individually and collectively, to the history of nursing and hospital founding has only recently begun to be recognized. Too often the Grey Nuns are the victims of sensational literature that reduce them to dim-witted, ruler-wielding, sexually frustrated beings. The "good sister" cringes at the sight of male Ecclesiastical authority and retreats behind her walled convent to starve and pray herself into heaven. Or she chooses the faith-filled path to a sacrificial life, as succinctly described by Mother M. John Hughes, the first Superior of the Aberdeen Presentation Sisters: "We offer you no salary: no recompense: no holidays; no pensions, but much hard work; a poor dwelling; few consolations; many disappointments, frequent sickness; a violent or lonely death."[7] Such a life held little resemblance to the actual behavior, goals and accomplishments of a Grey Nun in Lewiston, Maine.

And finally, the Grey Nuns persevered despite the formidable obstacles posed by their immigrant status, Yankee anti-Catholicism and widespread gender bias. The sisters' desire to have their health and child care ministries succeed required them to establish their own boundaries and achieve new self-understandings. A woman who joined the Grey Nun order was not restricted to a life behind convent walls, as in some religious orders, or the reality of grueling domesticity accompanied with continuous childbearing that characterized a significant percentage of the nineteenth-century female immigrant experience. Rather the life of a Grey Nun, while physically demanding, was one of continual education, professional opportunities, and personal and communal success.

Chapter One
"Everyone was poor"

On April 8th 1902, a crowd of 10,000 gathered in the city of Lewiston to celebrate the official blessing of the Grey Nuns' latest hospital facility by the Most Reverend Bishop William O'Connell. Not until 1908 would the foundation's formal name, the Hospital General Sainte-Marie, a name that blended both its English and French heritage, become widely used. The Lewiston community of Grey Nuns had founded a three-story brick hospital built of 980,000 bricks and 640 yards of stone work. It contained 150 beds divided into twelve wards, with an additional twenty-five bassinets in a new maternity ward. Sainte-Marie had fixtures for both gas and electricity with steel ceiling and even an elevator well constructed by the Penn Metal Ceiling and Roofing Co., from Philadelphia. There were two Gurney heaters each with a 9,000-foot capacity set by Henri Lagassey. The heating system required one ton of coal per day. The responsibility for obtaining such quantities of coal in an unstable market received the comment "Poor Sisters!" in the hospital's annual report. Once again the assumption was made that the Grey Nuns would simply find a way to acquire affordable coal. The official cost for the hospital was reported to have been $100,000, collected penny by penny as the Grey Nuns' begged, toiled, nursed, taught and cared. This sum, however excluded the twenty-three years of unpaid labor, sacrifice and prayers by the community.[1]

In 1902 both the hospital and the Lewiston community of Grey Nuns were under the authority of a new Superior, Sister Mary of the Incarnation. As a woman religious belonging to the congregation of Saint-Hyacinthe Grey Nuns, Sister Mary of the Incarnation lived a life that embodied an outwardly focused vocation that aggressively and consistently practiced charity. Regardless of external challenges, such as obtaining large quantities of coal, as a Grey Nun, Sister Mary educated herself and adapted Sainte-Marie to bring the best medical care of the time to the victims of nineteenth-century industrialization and urbanization.

The urgency and realism that defined her leadership was guided by the model of the Christ of her faith and the founder of her congregation, Saint Marguerite d'Youville. As the Lewiston Mother Superior, Sister Mary was responsible for the corporal and spiritual needs of her community, the hospital and the girls' orphanage. The boy's orphanage, the Healy Asylum, had its own Grey Nun superior who ran the institution independently. Sister Mary's skills as an administrator, pharmacist, healer, and bilingual communicator successfully drove the expansion of both the community and its social welfare medical ministry in Lewiston.

Sister Mary of the Incarnation was born Honorine Brodeur on January 18, 1864 in the village of Saint Antoine located outside of Montreal, Quebec. Her father was a farmer. Of the Grey Nuns who came to Lewiston and worked in the community from 1878 to 1908, 63 percent of the sisters listed their father's occupation as farmer. The next largest percentage of employment was listed as merchant at 6 percent.

Sister Mary's uncle and cousin, however, had left the rural life of a Quebecois farmer and were both successful physicians and surgeons in Montreal. As a child Honorine Brodeur had the privilege to receive a formal convent education in the city of Saint Denis from the sisters of the Congregation of Notre Dame. Brodeur entered the religious life in 1884 at the age of twenty. She was the 203rd woman to dedicate her life as a member of the Saint-Hyacinthe community of Grey Nuns since the order's founding in 1840 by Mother Marie-Michel Archange Thuot. The year Brodeur entered the convent at Saint-Hyacinthe, seventeen other young women would also be accepted as Grey Nun novices. Brodeur was the fourth novice received into the order for the year 1884. She made her final profession on August 2, 1886, beginning her life as a Grey Nun, known forevermore as Sister Mary of the Incarnation.[2]

Two years later Sister Mary, at the age of twenty-four, was sent to Lewiston and assigned as the pharmacist in the Grey Nuns' first hospital foundation, the Asylum of Our Lady of Lourdes. She was also given a teaching position at Saint Pierre's parochial school that was located in the Dominican Block. In 1892 the Grey Nun Superior relieved her of teaching responsibilities.[3] Now assigned to only hospital work, Sister Mary began an intensive medical training that would lead to a distinguished career as a medical professional.

For over fourteen years the Grey Nuns' annals recorded that Sister Mary participated in every medical and surgical procedure performed at the Asylum of Our Lady of Lourdes.[4] The precise details of Sister Mary's involvement have not been preserved. But what can be surmised is that her professional responsibilities would have been similar to that of an active medical intern. Using her knowledge as a sister-nurse and pharmacist she was a valuable contributor in a patient's healing process. To draw a comparison between Sister Mary's informal medical training and our contemporary academically rigorous medical standards would be absurd. Yet Sister Mary invested over twice the amount of time involved in actual hospital patient care than required by our current standards to be licensed as a physician. Furthermore, a Board of Licensure in Medicine was not established in Maine until 1895, three years after Sister Mary finished her training period at the Asylum of Our Lady of Lourdes.[5] Moreover, both her gender and faith tradition during her lifetime, prevented her from seeking formal and equal acceptance into the emerging male elite-controlled medical profession. Sister Mary's intensive hands-on hospital patient training however testifies that acquiring the skills and knowledge to provide professionalized medical care was of critical and foremost importance to a Grey Nun in her hospital training.

Sister Mary was fluent in both English and French. Under her first term as Superior at Sainte-Marie, 1902–1907, the use of the English language began to be implemented in the order's internal hospital documents used in the Lewiston community. She concluded her first term as Superior of Hospital General Sainte-Marie with the establishment of an in-hospital "Training School for Lay Nurses." The school opened the following year in 1908 "in a classroom prepared for that purpose" and proceeded to educate young women in the profession of nursing for the next eighty years.[6] A similar nursing school had been established six years prior at the motherhouse in Saint-Hyacinthe.

Instruction in the nursing school was conducted in both English and French with classes on "the theory and practice of nursing" that were taught by "a graduate of eleven years of experience in this line of work," from the Grey Nuns' motherhouse in Saint-Hyacinthe. There were nine women accepted into the first class who were supervised by two sister-nurses. The "pupil nurses" were not permitted to "work among the patients. . . . except under the supervision of the Sisters trained in the work." It was a two year and three month training program with lectures in "anatomy, physiology, bacteriology and hygiene, medical, surgical, gynecological and ophthalmologic nursing." These lectures were delivered by Sainte-Marie's medical and surgical staff.[7]

Sister Mary structured the lay nursing training school to parallel the educational standards and institutional treatment in a Grey Nun novitiate. Like a young postulant who desired admittance as a Grey Nun novice, a woman who desired acceptance into the lay nursing school had a three-month probation period. According to the nursing school stipulations:

"During this period, board and lodging will be provided, but no other compensation. The deportment and attitudes of probationers are under close scrutiny, a written record of notable points being kept. At the expiration of probationary term, the authorities of the hospital decide upon the fitness of each candidate. If admitted she will be required to remain two-years in the school, and to conform to the rules, not only in the letter but also in the spirit of the house."[8]

The two years of training which was required of the lay nurse, parallels the two year period when a women was accepted into the Grey Nun community until she made her first vows. The structural design of the nursing school to mirror the Grey Nuns' novitiate was extended to include that the chain of command was equally shared by professional medical authority and the Grey Nun Mother Superior. When the nursing pupil passed her final exams, her diploma was signed both by "the President and Secretary of the Medical Board" and the Grey Nun "Mother Superior, and the sister Superintendent of Nurses."[9]

By integrating a formal nursing school into the Hospital General Sainte-Marie complex, the Grey Nun leadership acknowledged that professional training was vital to the success of their medical mission. Yet the Grey Nuns did not abdicate their authority over these women to the secular and male-controlled Medical Boards. As clearly written by the signatures on the nurse's diploma she was equally responsible to the Grey Nuns' Mother Superior and her supervising sister-nurses as to the President and Secretary of the Medical Board.[10]

Despite Sister Mary's medical acumen, professional achievements, and position of leadership, she apparently never sought personal recognition. What she did seek and achieve was to improve the conditions of both the suffering poor in her hospital and those of her religious sisters. A single letter has been preserved in the Portland Chancery Archives that illustrates Sister Mary's determination to improve facilities at her hospital.

In this letter dated April 9, 1903, Sister Mary asked the Portland Chancery for formal permission to accept a State grant. Since the hospital had already accepted State funding, this letter was a polite acknowledgment by the hospital's Superior of Church protocol and their status as a guest community within his diocese. Sister Mary wrote to the bishop that:

"When the delegation [of State Officials] came over they went to see the place where we do our washing and ironing. All were astonished to see such a poor place, so they told me, we shall grant you some money

to equip and build a decent Laundry. So you will not [be] oblige[d] to
go into the snow to spread your cloth[es]."[11]

This letter refers to the practice of spreading wet clothes onto the
frozen ground or snow to allow them to freeze dry. Then the sister would
collect the frozen clothing and quickly snap the article to shatter the ice
from the material, leaving it damp but clean. One can only imagine the difficulties associated with this process and how valuable a "decent laundry"
would have been to the sisters. A view that Sister Mary clearly expressed in
her closing words: "this is the most important thing to have."[12]

While the letter was written in somewhat affected language, it testifies
to Sister Mary's ambition to improve the minimal conditions that defined
not only her community's life, but also that of her patients. The Grey Nuns
and their patients equally shared the harshness of urban survival in their
industrially transformed urban environment. Yet while Sister Mary's religious self-understanding may have led to the reframing of her patients' suffering to a covenant relationship between the Grey Nuns, their patients and
their God, she did not turn her administration of Hospital General Sainte-
Marie into an act of blind trust in Providence.[13] Rather her leadership mirrored a ministry of action that benefited her religious community, patients,
and especially Lewiston's poor. The following chapter will explore the first
years of the Grey Nuns' ministry in Lewiston. These first sisters laid the
foundation that would grow into the Hospital General Sainte-Marie, in less
than three decades.

Chapter Two
An Autumn Arrival

Their journey began with a train ride. On November 20, 1878 three Quebecois Grey Nuns arrived in Lewiston via the Grand Trunk Railroad from
Saint-Hyacinthe, Quebec. The Grey Nuns came to Lewiston at the
request of the Lewiston priest Reverend Pierre Hevey, a native of Saint-
Hyacinthe. Hevey had entered the diocesan Seminary of Saint-Hyacinthe
in 1850 and was ordained to the Catholic priesthood at the age of
twenty-six on July 12, 1857. Following two assignments to parishes in
Quebec, Hevey migrated to the United States, joining the Portland Diocese in October 11, 1871. He was directly sent to Lewiston from Portland
to replace the Reverend Edouard Letourneau as the pastor of the French
Canadian church Saint Pierre by Portland Bishop David Bacon. Hevey
became a dynamic economic and religious leader of Lewiston's expanding
French Canadian population for the next ten years. He was a principal
supporter of the Grey Nuns' social welfare and medical ministry through
out his life. Hevey was transferred to Manchester, New Hampshire by
Portland Bishop James Healy in 1881 where he remained until his death
in 1910.[1]

While Hevey's position as the spiritual leader to Lewiston's French
Canadians gave him the moral authority to guide the community's
growth, it was his entrepreneurial talents as a financier which empow-
ered the immigrant French Canadian community. His business acumen
secured his authority as the community's leader, while simultaneously
expanding the resources he could wield. Hevey's personal wealth would
eventually come to play a significant role in the early financing of the
Grey Nuns' hospital. Despite Hevey's success, within six years he
encountered a ministerial crisis that presented a significant obstacle to
his parish community.

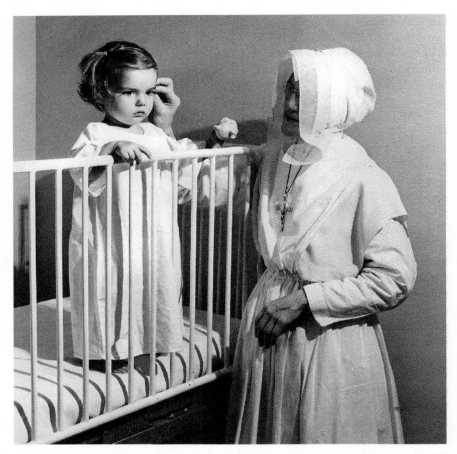

Figure 1: Sister Martel, Chief of Pediatrics, and One of Her Patients.

The French Canadian Catholic population of Lewiston was expanding at a rate of 12 percent annually from 1880 to 1900, as measured by the population growth of their national parish, Saint Pierre. The immigrants' need for social services and bilingual education was acute. Hevey had to find a way to provide these services without unduly burdening his parish with debt. Hevey met this challenge, as many of his nineteenth-century brethren did, by soliciting the skills and free labor of a congregation of women religious, who were often immigrants themselves.

Hevey wrote to the Saint-Hyacinthe Grey Nuns' Superior General in 1877 requesting that the Grey Nuns come to Lewiston and minister to "a Canadian congregation to do classes [teach] and to visit the poor in their homes."[2] According to the Grey Nuns' annals Hevey's letter received a favorable response on September 13th from the Superior General and the order's counsel: "It was decided today in the assembly that the administration of the community would accept the Lewiston mission and that the Superior herself would go visit the mission. The Superior would make the arrangements with Rev. Hevey for the condition of this new foundation."[3]

The acceptance of Hevey's request by the Grey Nuns of Saint-Hyacinthe represented the initial step towards the establishment of a medical and welfare institution that would be under their authority for the next century. Not until January 1992 was the sponsorship of Saint Mary's General Hospital and associated facilities transferred to The Sisters of Charity of Montreal, Grey Nuns, as a member organization of Covenant Health Systems, Inc. of Lexington, Massachusetts.[4]

Hevey's invitation to this particular community of French Canadian women religious was not accidental. As a native of Saint-Hyacinthe, Hevey knew of the Grey Nuns' expertise as sister-nurses. However, the Grey Nuns' constitution does not identify them as a community dedicated to academic pursuits, which led to a conflict in their Lewiston mission. Every religious congregation, both male and female, has a written constitution that has been either approved by the Vatican or by the local diocese. An order's constitution is a single or collection of documents, which detail the precise ministry and unique spirituality that defines one religious community from another. The Grey Nuns' constitution does not emphasize an educational ministry directed to youth. Lewiston eventually became the recipient of two additional congregations of immigrant women religious who were foremost educators unlike the Grey Nuns. They were the French Dominican Sisters of Nancy and the Sisters of Sion from Canada. Both of these congregations would establish foundations in Lewiston and Auburn to educate French Canadian children. The French Canadian congregation of the Sisters of Sion was in Lewiston and Auburn from 1892–1904. The Dominican Sisters of Nancy arrived in Lewiston in 1904 and remain there today. Their current convent is located in the town of Sabbatus, which is adjacent to Lewiston.

While the Sisters of Sion had only a brief twelve-year ministry in the Twin Cities of Lewiston and Auburn, their impact was significant. Eighty-one young women entered their Maine novitiate with sixty-five making a final profession prior to the order's departure. The Sisters of Sion withdrew from Maine for reasons still unclear. One possible explanation is that the Dominican priests who became the Spiritual leaders of the Lewiston French Canadian community by the twentieth century, failed to fulfill their original agreement that the Sisters of Sion were to be relieved from teaching boys of high school age. The breaking of this promise which had been agreed upon by the Dominican priests prior to the Sisters of Sions' acceptance of a Maine mission was a violation to the order's teaching ministry.

Due to their constitution, the Sisters of Sion were not permitted to teach boys after the primary grades. To this congregation, these students were judged to be men, and thus required adult male teachers not women religious. By 1904 the failure of the Dominican priests to resolve this situation created an irreconcilable tension in their Maine ministry. In addition to this untenable situation, another possible reason for the Sions' departure was that the General Council of the Congregation, at that time, was located in Paris, France. Geographically separated from the dynamics of the Maine situation by the Atlantic Ocean, the congregation's leadership would have lacked direct and expedient communication to make a fully informed decision on the fate of their Lewiston daughters.[5]

Unlike the Sisters of Sion, the Grey Nuns, perhaps due to their vow of obedience and desire to expand their ministry, felt impelled to accept Hevey's request even though they had little, if any, expertise in parochial educational endeavors. Their involvement in educational insitutions will be discussed in Chapter Nine. Yet the placing of women religious into professional positions for which they had only minimal, if any, training was a common practice in the American church. Usually a sister was placed in a parochial school with the only requirement being that she be the same ethnic background as her students. These women worked essentially for free, as the clergy needed teachers for their overcrowded schools; the poverty of women religious was of secondary importance. The sister's lack of professional resources and support coupled with the necessity of on the job learning has contributed to inaccurate and often cruel tales of "ugly sister stories" that characterize sensationalized accounts in American Catholic lore.

Another interpretation for the Grey Nuns' openness to Hevey's invitation and their willingness to help Lewiston's suffering poor, despite constitutional restrictions, was that his request mirrored the order's religious self-understanding. As the spiritual daughters of their founder Saint Marguerite d'Youville they embraced the diversity of needs that defines charitable work. The sisters' desire to expand their order into Lewiston furthermore belonged to a paradigmatic evangelical movement in the American religious scene, which occurred during the second part of the nineteenth century. As many feminist scholars, including Sioban Nelson, Janet Wilson James, and Linda Gordon, have argued, both religious and secular leadership searched out single women, vowed women and/or communities of Catholic women religious to work in rural settle-ment and urban centers.[6] Their assigned task was to establish comprehen-sive benevolent institutions to care for and serve the proletariat as America simultaneously underwent industrialization and transformed from a rural culture into an urban society. This task, furthermore, was to be achieved by these women with minimal financial support from the male religious, polit-ical and secular elite.

The economic system of nineteenth-century capitalism which pro-pelled American industrialization was profit driven. During the nineteenth-century, the American Catholic church was an impoverished institution that was ethnically divided and socially marginalized. Unlike the culturally rooted and politically supported Protestant benevolent structures that were emerging during the late nineteenth century, the American Catholic church had limited economic or political resources. The Catholic hierarchy, faced with the dynamics of minimal resources and an exploding illiterate or non-English speaking, immigrant population, turned to the free labor of foreign and domestic Catholic women religious. These women were either requested or assigned to provide education, medical care, and social serv-ices in geographical and national parishes to a fragmented Catholic dias-pora. It must be noted that single Catholic immigrant women who remained secular had little time for extensive involvement in structured benevolence. Their domestic labor and earnings were essential if their fam-ily was to avoid starvation or deprivation. What these secular women did do, however, was generously donate their hard earned money to their parish collection plates. Penny by penny, these women's offerings financed the construction of Catholic institutions that altered the landscape of urban America and transformed the nation's welfare system.

National parishes offered the familiar to their immigrant congrega-tions, through a network of religious and institutional welfare services and structures administered by local community members, clergy or religious sisters usually of a similar ethnic or linguistic background. As Thomas Philpott argues, these ethnically operated welfare structures allowed immi-grants the freedom to "control" their own "Americanization process."[7] Among French Canadians and other immigrants, the retention of the native language was often essential to their self-respect. This need was honored in the national parish structures. Herve-B. LeMaire has argued that French Canadians tenaciously fought to "speak French natively . . . compared with most other immigrant languages in the United States [and] survives with surprising vigor." LeMaire credits this achievement to "the determined efforts of the first Franco-Americans, who had the vision to establish a vast network of interlocking religious, educational, cultural, and fraternal organizations at a relatively early date."[8] The central organization of any French Canadian community in New England was the national parish. The sociologists C.J. Nuesse and Thomas Harte interpret the national parishes as in fact being "synonymous with a foreign language group."[9] In Lewiston's Saint Pierre church the French language was central to the parish culture and the community at large. Yet, as Philip Gleason reminds us, the value of language was not the only means for immigrants to preserve their religious heritage. Rather Gleason believes that "language, religion, and culture interpenetrated each other so thoroughly that it was impossible to think of them separately."[10]

It must be acknowledged that the acceptance of French within Lewiston by non-French Canadian Catholics and clergy was not reflective of official policy among the North American bishops during the nineteenth century. In fact the Catholic hierarchy took an aggressive approach to Americanize and the assimilation of non-English-speaking ethnicities into the English-speaking American. This position was bluntly stated by the Reverend James E. Cassidy in September 1905: "The grandeur of a nation depends upon the assimilation of the diverse races that come to live in that country."[11]

The pro-assimilation position which the American bishops professed was aided by the lack of available foreign language speaking clergy; Lewiston was no exception. As seen by Bishop David Bacon's decision to implement a North American wide search in 1870 to find Reverend Edouard Letourneau, the Quebecois predecessor to Reverend Pierre Hevey. When the Grey Nuns arrived in 1878, Hevey was the sole priest for a congregation of 3,500 communicants at Saint Pierre. Despite the magnitude of his responsibility, some social services were beginning to be established for the parishioners of Saint Pierre, such as Hevey's fledgling credit union, but medical and welfare aid was urgently needed by the community. While the national parish was recognized from within the community as a safe and familiar haven, the absence of skilled labor to provide sustainable welfare, educational and medical care services left the immigrant and poor stagnating in their plight. Inviting a congregation of Quebecois Catholic women religious to come to Lewiston represented to the clergy and local leaders the most economically practical and culturally sensitive alternative.

Furthermore, the Catholic poor benefited from the sisters' approach to the reality of poverty. The sisters did not treat the poor with condescending attitudes or judgment, but rather attached a spiritual dimension to their plight. Dorothy M. Brown and Elizabeth McKeown both argue that Catholic leadership claimed that America's poor "belonged" to the Catholic Church.[12] It was a fundamental mission of the American church

to alleviate either the causes or the condition of poverty that were con-
demning the poor to early deaths in slums, mills, mines and sweatshops.
The Catholic poor were instructed to turn to the church and her institutions for aid rather then the secular welfare agencies that were under the
domain of federal or Protestant authorities. The development of this ideol-
ogy in the American church was paralleled in the Grey Nuns' religious self-
understanding of their welfare and medical ministry in Lewiston.

THE FIRST LEWISTON COMMUNITY

Who were these Quebecois women religious that stepped off the Grand
Trunk Railroad train into a new country? They were Sister Adeline Le
Blanc, Sister Rosalie Galipeau, and Sister Alponsine Cote.[13] Le Blanc was
thirty-four years old and had worked as a Grey Nun in both Manitoba and
at the Saint-Elizabeth Hospice in Farham, Quebec. She would become the
Superior of the Asylum of Our Lady of Lourdes in Lewiston in 1892. This
medical facility was the foundation of Hospital General Sainte-Marie. Galipeau was thirty-one years old and was from a farming background. Cote
was the oldest member of the tiny community at forty-eight and came from
an educated family. Her father identified himself as a member of the French
Canadian bourgeois. Cote had worked at two Grey Nun institutions previously: the Hospital General in Sorel, Quebec, and, the Hospice of the
Sacred Heart in Sherbrooke, Quebec. She was selected by the order's constitutional electoral process to be the Superior of the new foundation in
Lewiston. Cote held this office until the Grey Nuns' health care ministry in
Lewiston became a reality. She returned to Saint-Hyacinthe in 1887
remaining there until her death in 1911 at the age of eighty-one.

Within a month of their arrival, this tiny band of religious would
grow through the addition of two sisters, Sisters Philomena Champoux and
Corinne Frederic, both sent from Saint-Hyacinthe.[14] The sisters traveled via
train to Lewiston without the company of clergy. Many nineteenth-century
women religious enjoyed the ability to travel openly in American secular
society as they pursued their benevolent works. This freedom was dramatically curtailed by the 1917 Canon Law re-codification. As detailed in the
order's accounting book, various modes of travel were used to mitigate
expenses; the benefit of shared experience and education was so valued by
the order that cost was of secondary importance but thrift was always a
priority to the community. For example in 1884 the Lewiston community
paid the sum of $7.50 "for the travel of Sister of the Sacred-Heart"
between Lewiston and Saint-Hyacinthe. In addition to the expense of her
travel the community paid another $3.00 for "various" costs.

There is a paucity of personal information about the individual women who were collectively the Grey Nuns. When a sister died, the order's chronicler might or might not record the sister's accomplishments and location of ministry in a private community obituary. The content of the sisters' obituaries were neither recorded in a consistent manner nor made available to the non-religious or general public. Only immediate family members might have received a copy of the sister's obituary. Furthermore, the lack of surviving information on individual sisters was compounded by the use of both French and English versions of names and by the practice of changing birth and family names to a Roman Catholic saint's name when a woman professed as a Grey Nun. For example, the first Superior of Hospital General Sainte-Marie was known in the Lewiston community as Sister Mary of the Incarnation. But in Saint-Hyacinthe she used the French translation of her name and went by Soeur Marie de l'Incarnation. Her birth name was Honorine Brodeur which she never used following her profession as a Grey Nun on August 2, 1886.

The community's annals, however, can be effectively used if the information is viewed similarly as a topographical map that illustrates general shapes and significant characteristics of its subject rather than an intimate detailed picture. In general, the annals contain the broad unfolding story of the order, peppered with specific events or action, of an individual sister or foundation of the Grey Nuns' communal history. The section of the Grey Nuns' annals that was written during the last decades of the nineteenth century takes on a testimonial form. It was meant for private reading, by only other Grey Nuns, not for public readership. The annals are a written reflection of the Grey Nuns' commitment to live as a consecrated community of nursing-sisters and the dangers and glories entailed in that effort. What emerges from the pages is a fascinating story of how the Grey Nuns succeeded despite numerous and formidable obstacles that challenged their ministry and often cost them their health and/or life. The annals testify that the success of the Grey Nuns was dependent upon open dialogue between communities, the motherhouse, and the leadership of the Superior General. The emphasis on communication and supportive involvement by the order's leadership protected both the Grey Nuns' unique religious identity and independent structures. Moreover, the sharing of information among diverse ministries created an environment were adaptation within Grey Nun communities was valued. As noted in the Superior General's reports on her visits to Lewiston, she sometimes imposed discipline for infractions of the order's rule. Yet the Superior General also supported innovative changes to the rule to accommodate particular difficulties or specific goals of the Lewiston mission.

For example in her 1892 report the Superior General wrote: "From now on we will ring the sleeping bell at 9:30 P.M. without ringing the prescribed dongs as determined in the rule. So as not to disturb the ill patients who are very close to the sister's regular apartments."[12] In 1900 the Superior General recognized the "excessive fatigue" of the sisters and altered the rule by allowing the sisters to "recite the rosary in one chorus."[13] By 1902 the Superior General took the radical step and permitted the sisters to "observe half-silence in the large hallways. That is to say we shall be able to speak in a soft voice for necessary and practical things." Furthermore this year she granted the local superior the authority to "extend the right to speak in the refectory on days off, dinners, suppers, plus twenty other meals of her choice."[15]

In addition to mentoring, the Grey Nuns' leadership also valued practical planning to ensure humane treatment of a new community. This was evident prior to the Grey Nuns' formal acceptance of Hevey's request that they come to Lewiston. As recorded in the annals, the Mother Superior and her council demanded that Reverend Hevey detail the conditions of the lodgings he had acquired for the sisters before they departed Saint-Hyacinthe. This was prompted by practical concerns that the sisters were not placed by local clergy in unacceptable lodging upon their arrival in Lewiston as many other communities were. Hevey wrote in response to the Mother Superior on September 20, 1878:

> "In response to your request, here is what I have been able to establish as a house for your order in Lewiston.
>
>   I will give a lot of land by 100 feet by 50 feet on the corners of Pierce and Walnut Street. On this lot two houses of wood are located which I will unite with a passage for easier access. The first house is about 22 feet long 20 feet wide with an addition of 18 feet. The second house is 25 by 22 feet. This last house has two stories and the other one has one and a half stories. I commit myself for the first year to furnish to the sisters what could be lacking towards their expenses for the year."[16]

Despite Hevey's reassurances the condition of this dwelling was poor. It lacked insulation and adequate furniture and was too small for the mission the Grey Nuns had envisioned. Furthermore, when the Grey Nuns began residence at the Pierce and Walnut property, they also assumed the financial obligation for the property. According to the property deed registered on April 25, 1879 in the City of Lewiston Register of Deeds at the Androscoggin Country Courthouse, the sisters accepted financial responsibility for the property if success of their ministry was not achieved. These harsh terms were not a surprise to the sisters. Financial abuse of women religious by both the secular public and their own Catholic clergy was not uncommon in the nineteenth and early twentieth centuries. In fact, Hevey had closed his letter by noting the mortgage that the Grey Nuns must assume if they failed in Lewiston: "In case you should abandon this apostolate for which the house has been founded. You [the Grey Nuns] shall pay to the Bishop costs employed for your works of Charity in Lewiston."[17]

By the end of their first year in Lewiston, however the Grey Nuns had not failed. In fact they had become the "Asylum of Our Lady of Lourdes, a corporation for Benevolent, Charitable and Educational Purposes," organized under the laws of the State of Maine as recorded in the Lewiston City Register in the Androscoggin County Courthouse. Perhaps as a sign of faith, this name, The Asylum of Our Lady of Lourdes, had been selected by the order's council before the first sisters departed for Lewiston from Saint-Hyacinthe.

When these deeds were signed, the Grey Nuns were a French speaking community in an English speaking country. They were a female order of poor French Canadian Catholics living in an industrial city controlled by an elite minority of prosperous male and female Yankees. Nevertheless as their actions and the documents testify, they remained in Lewiston as an independent order of women religious determined to live an apostolic life of charity, benevolence, and education.

In the following chapter an overview of the unique culture of Maine and the sociological and industrial environment which dominated the textile city of Lewiston prior to the Grey Nuns' arrival is provided. It is of fundamental importance to examine this material in order to fully grasp the societal and economic complexities which the Grey Nuns encountered. Understanding these complexities is necessary for insight into the Grey Nuns' behavior and the magnitude of their charitable achievements.

Chapter Three
The Transformation of Nineteenth-Century Maine

The State of Maine is perhaps the most isolated of the contiguous American states. It is bordered on the northwest by the Canadian province of Quebec and on the northeast by the Canadian province of New Brunswick. Both Quebec and New Brunswick were territories of New France until the British Conquest on September 18, 1759. British sovereignty, however, was not firmly established until the Treaty of Paris in 1763, which gave England control over the majority of French territory in North America. Maine's south and southeastern border are the salty waters of the Atlantic Ocean. The coastal line of the state is elongated and irregular; the result is over 2,400 miles of shoreline. The state's only shared border with another American state is its western boundary with New Hampshire.

Maine contains 33,215 square miles, which almost equals the combined size of the remaining New England states. There are approximately 2,500 lakes and over 5,000 rivers and streams that crisscross the state. Of the six largest rivers, only the Saint John and its tributaries drain north of the central divide. Harsh winters characterized by interior snowfalls of one hundred inches and a mean winter temperature of twenty degrees Fahrenheit created a settlement pattern of small isolated townships. Forest still covers almost four-fifths of the state. Maine's geography had fostered the economic development of three distinct industries by the industrial age: fish and maritime; timber and wood products; and textile and shoe manufacturing.

In the latter part of the nineteenth-century the central to southeastern portion of the state was marked by manufacturing and industrial development, which coincided with an expanding population, an agricultural crisis, and a shortage of wage work in rural Quebec. The dynamics of this situation would eventually lead to the altering of the ethnic composition of

Figure 2: The Great Falls of the Androscoggin; Lewiston's mills in background.

Maine's population, with the predominant minority becoming French Canadian by the turn of the twentieth century. The industrialization and subsequent ethnic change of Maine was directly influenced by the drainage of five
major rivers and their tributaries, which provided significant hydroelectric
power resources to industries for the development of textile production.

In the city of Lewiston in 1836, local entrepreneurs formed the
Androscoggin Falls Mill, Dam, Locks, and Canal Company to harness the
hydro-energy of the Great Falls, located directly above Lewiston and its
twin city Auburn. Following the nationwide financial panic of 1837, this
company would be reorganized as the Lewiston Falls Cotton Mill in early
1845. Later that year, the Lewiston Falls Cotton Mill investors joined with
investors from Boston, Pawtucket, and Lawrence to organize the Lewiston
Water Power Company, which, in turn, became the Franklin Company. In
addition to the power rights of the Great Falls on the Androscoggin River,
the Franklin Company also came to own much of the real estate which then
comprised the cities of Lewiston and Auburn. Furthermore, individuals and
corporations could only buy or lease water rights from the Franklin Company. This meant that the Franklin Company profited from a tripartite
monopoly over energy resources, real estate and industrial production in
nineteenth-century Lewiston.

In the city of Auburn industrial growth was primarily in shoe production. There were two small shoe factories in Auburn in 1836. With the arrival of the railroad in Auburn in 1849, the industry exploded. By 1859, twenty-three shoe factories were established that produced an estimated 271,200 pairs of shoes a year with an approximate payroll of $400,000.[1] Employment in the nineteenth-century shoe industry was not stable due to technological advancement, such as the shoe-lasting machine which was invented in 1882, replacing the need for human labor.[2] In 1876 the Auburn shoe industry employed 3,000 wage-laborers but by 1886 the need for labor had been reduced to a work force of 1,500. Yet nine years later the shoe industry had regained its strength and employed about 2,000 with an estimated payroll of $850,000.[3] Despite the unstable market conditions in the shoe industry, French Canadian immigrants were nevertheless continually attracted to Auburn to work in the shoe industry. These immigrants formed a small French Canadian community which was a satellite to Lewiston's Petit Canada. When the French Canadian national parish of Saint Louis was established in 1902, this community gained the distinction of having its own parish and church, which secured its separate identity from Lewiston; albeit thirty-two years after the founding of Lewiston's own French Canadian Parish, Saint Pierre.[4]

In 1849–1850, construction began on the canal of the Lewiston Water Power Company (LWPC). The completion date for the canal is a matter of historical debate. Despite this lack of clarity, the significance of the canal to Lewiston's industrial development can not be overstated. Upon the canal's completion the two parallel and several cross canals and granite locks at the head of the main canal created an efficient hydraulic power and hydroelectric network. This system increased both the availability and effectiveness of the Androscoggin River to power the expanding industrial center on Lewiston's river front. The system extended for three-fourths of a mile, and was fourteen feet deep and sixty-two feet wide at the top, narrowing to fifty-eight feet at the bottom.

To establish the precise founding dates and names of the various Lewiston's mills is problematic. The names, dates, and interrelationships between these facilities form, especially after more than a hundred years, a dense and confusing web. The complexity of this web led the Bates College scholars A. M. Myhrman and J. A. Rademaker to conclude in their socio-economic study of Lewiston-Auburn that "the relationship . . . between the Lewiston Water-Power Company, the Franklin Company, and the individual mill companies are not easily unraveled."[5] As revealed in the corporate evolution of the LWPC into the Franklin Company, mill sites repeatedly changed names and ownership. This practice was unique neither to this period nor the textile industry; it continues to be characteristic of Maine's last mill-based industry, forest products. For example, in rural central Maine in the late 1900s, the Rumford Falls Paper Company became the Rumford Falls Sulfite Company. Both companies were purchased by International Paper Company in 1898 and incorporated as Oxford Paper Company. The Ethyl Corporation purchased Oxford Paper Company in 1967, and sold it to the Boise Cascade Corporation in 1976. Boise Cascade sold the mill to the Mead Corporation in 1996. Mead then merged with Westvaco in 2002 becoming the MeadWestvaco Corporation. In 2005 MeadWestvaco sold the mill to an independent group of investors and it became the Rumford Paper Company. The mill facilities have never changed location and generations of Maine families have worked at the mill which they refer to simply as "the Rumford mill."

Furthermore, while corporate ownership of Maine's mills is traceable, there is a lack of consensus on the precise dates of the various mills due to confusion over the time when full operation was achieved versus the date of establishment. This ambiguity has been enhanced as the textile industry in Maine declined over the last decades of the twentieth century. Several mill sites were eventually closed leaving their operational records and archives abandoned or destroyed.

Recognizing the inherent ambiguity associated with the founding dates and names of Lewiston's mills, the following list of dates and names is as accurate as surviving documents permit.[6] The first mill to be founded in Lewiston during the nineteenth century was the Lincoln Mill which started operations in 1846, and had several later additions. Perhaps the most famous mill was the Bates Mill. Within the Bates complex, Mill Number One was built in 1850/52, Mill Number Two in 1854, and Mill Number Three in 1868. By the late 1880s, this complex employed an estimated 3,000 people. The Hill Manufacturing Company opened its Mill Number One in 1854 and Number Two in 1864; both employed approximately 700 workers each.[7]

The Androscoggin Company established its first mill in 1861, and it quickly became one of the biggest cotton mills in America. The Androscoggin Company continued to expand and built two additional mills, one in 1867 and the other five years later in 1872. The Porter Mill was built in 1858 and became the Continental Mill in 1872; the Avon Mill and the Cumberland Mill were both established in the mid-nineteen hundreds but the exact dates are unknown. There were also several bleacheries established in Lewiston to supply the mills, the first of these opened in 1860.[8]

The rapid rate of Lewiston's industrial development was dependent not only upon the availability of cheap energy, but also on cheap wage labor. By the mid-nineteenth century the local rural Yankee population of Maine could not sustain Lewiston's industrial demands for labor. The

Figure 3: Mill Foreman and Workers.

resultant immigrant population boom from that point meant that until the industrial slowdown of the 1890s, Lewiston's population grew at a faster rate than Maine as a whole, with French Canadian immigrants dominating

the expansion. Over the fifteen years from 1876 to 1890, Lewiston's population grew almost ten times faster than the state, but within Lewiston, the
French Canadian population grew ten times faster than the city as a whole.

The Irish comprised the first wave of immigrant labor into Lewiston.
The dynamics of the French Canadian immigration into New England, however, challenged and then overwhelmed the Irish influx for textile mill work.
Catholic French Canadians who tenaciously clung to their own culture, faith
traditions and language, began a slow migration into New England's developing urban industrial centers starting in the 1850s.

Ralph Vicero has estimated that 300,000 French Canadians immigrated to the northeastern United States from 1850 to 1900.[9] This influx
contributed to the formation of social and economic boundaries due to the
lack of shared language skills between the immigrants and the previously
settled inhabitants. Furthermore, the socio-ethnic class distinctions inhib-
ited sharing of culture and knowledge between the two communities,
despite their shared urban environment. This migration dynamically
increased by the last decades of the century, greatly aided by the expanding
railroad network. The effects of this migration in Maine can be seen in the
demographic data for Androscoggin County and the cities of Lewiston and
Auburn from the U.S. Census of 1910. This census was taken at the very
end of the boom period in French Canadian immigration, and more than
twenty years after the Grey Nuns founded their hospital. However, unlike
prior censuses, this census contained more comprehensive information on

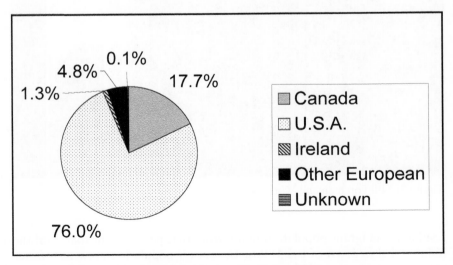

Figure 4: Nativity of Androscoggin County Residents, 1910.

the nationality of the county residents which gives, at worst, an underestimation of the impact of the French Canadian immigration.

Figure 4 shows the nationality of Androscoggin County in 1910. Representing the county's Yankee roots, the residents of Androscoggin County by 1910 were predominantly of British-American heritage with 76 percent of the population being native-born. However, a significant percentage of the county, 18 percent was from primarily French-speaking areas of Canada. Irish immigrants represented 1 percent of the county's population.

Turning to Lewiston and Auburn, the effect of the urban immigration to this area is clearly seen in Figure 5. The Twin Cities by 1910 had greater than 20 percent more Canadian residents than Androscoggin County, as a percent of the total, and twice the percentage of Irish origin. Even at this late date, the immigrant concentration in the Twin Cities was still apparent. More than 90 percent of the population in Androscoggin County hailing from these countries, lived in the Twin Cities.

The data for Lewiston is even more dramatic with regard to the large concentration of French Canadians. The 1910 data illustrated in Figure 6 shows that Lewiston had the same percentage of Irish and other European immigrants as both Lewiston and Auburn combined. This indicates that these cities had an equal distribution of Irish and other European immigrants. However, the significant concentration of French Canadian immigrants in Lewiston was revealed by the fact that Lewiston's percentage of Canadians was almost 33 percent higher than the Twin Cities combined. Given Lewiston's larger size, this means that Lewiston had more than three times the number of Canadian-born residents than Auburn, even at

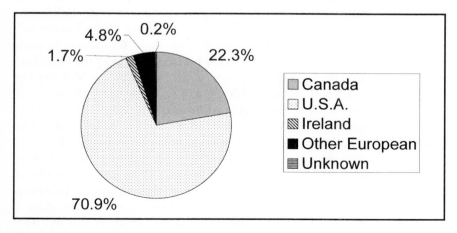

Figure 5: Nativity of Twin Cities Residents, 1910.

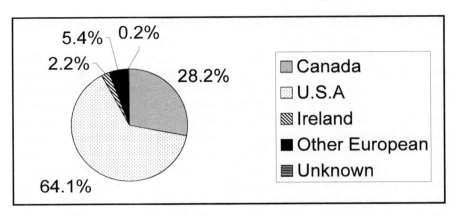

Figure 6: Nativity of Lewiston Residents, 1910.

this relatively late date in the French Canadian immigration to the area. In fact, this must be the lowest difference between the two cities since 1860, when the French Canadian immigration generally began. This is supported by an independent analysis that showed Lewiston's percentage of foreign-born residents was more than nine times that for Auburn in 1870.[10] By 1910, Lewiston only had twice as many foreign born residents than Auburn, as a percent of population.

Whether mill wage labor was secured by either immigrants or native born, the industry paid their laborers monthly and at discretion of the company director. This practice contributed to economic insecurity if any large unplanned expense occurred in the wage laborer's life and/or if any workplace conflict developed. In the city of Lewiston's 1883 Validation book, the following monthly schedule for "pay days of Corporations" was preserved. The Bates Mills payday was the third Wednesday of each month. The Hill Mill paid its laborers the first Tuesday after the third Saturday of each month. Both the Continental Mill and Lincoln Mill payday was on the 15th. The Lewiston Mill payday was the third Thursday of each month. The Bleachery paid its workforce on the 10th. The Lewiston Machine Company payday was on the 18th as was the Baker Mills. The Union Water Company met its payroll on the 20th.[11] The problematic nature of a four-week pay cycle would have victimized even the most frugal wage laborer and his or her family, especially if an unforeseen illness arose that prevented a return to work or required expensive medications. The hardships caused by this pay system led Maine to eventually adopt a statute requiring weekly pay for many industries, which is still in effect today.

In addition to the textile mills, Lewiston supported a variety of manufacturing companies and small businesses by the end of the nineteenth century. The prominent companies were: the Cowan Woolen Company, Lewiston Falls Manufacturing Company, and R. C. Pingree & Company. These companies each employed between 50 and 180 laborers annually. The majority of Lewiston's smaller ethnically owned family businesses, however, were French Canadian. Two examples of successful French Canadian businesses were the Alphonse Auger's Grocery store which opened in 1870 and F.X. Marcotte, Undertakers and Dealers in Furniture and Stoves founded in 1888. The Auger Grocery prospered and within a decade became the chief credit guarantor of the newly arrived French Canadians. Within half a century Marcotte became a significant benefactor to the Grey Nuns' hospital and child care foundations. In 1928 the company donated $120,000 to the Grey Nuns for the construction of a retirement home, Maison Marcotte, and a new orphanage, the Orphelinat Saint Joseph.[12]

The expansion of Lewiston's textile industry resulted in an acute labor shortage in the mills. As previously noted the first immigrant work force in Lewiston was ethnically dominated by Irish Catholics, who started arriving in the 1850s. The Irish immigrants in Lewiston, however, did not limit themselves to wage labor, but soon established independent contracting businesses, which directly contributed to the construction of Lewiston canal system and mills. This ethnic group quickly moved into other areas of employment, especially education, public service, and political activities. The practice of obtaining employment in public service and political activities was common for nineteenth-century Irish Americans. The combination of business investments and steady mill work enabled the Irish community to form "the first Catholic colony in Lewiston."[13] By 1857 Lewiston's Catholic colony was recognized by Portland's Bishop David Bacon as sufficiently stable to support a local parish. This resulted in the creation of Lewiston's first Catholic parish, Saint Joseph.

This secure source of Irish Catholic labor, however, was inadequate to meet the dynamic growth of Lewiston's textile industry. By the early 1870s there were seventeen corporations in Lewiston with an invested capital of $7,000,000 whose labor needs could not be met by the local population and existing immigrant wage-laborers.[14] Furthermore, mill operators judged that the Irish were "hard to manage as factory hands," and wanted a less "aggressive and easier to control" labor force to work in the nine cotton mills which ran more than 220,000 spindles by 1871.[15] A solution to the dynamic issues surrounding Lewiston's ethnic labor relations and shortage did exist in the international railroad system that had expanded from southern New England in 1849. The railroad had first enabled Lewiston's industry to prosper during the American Civil War by ending dependence on horse-drawn or small-scale water-borne transportation. In 1874, a spur line was opened which joined Lewiston to the northern rail system known as the Grand Trunk Railroad or the Canadian National Railway Line. By this connection Lewiston became a direct station for migrating French Canadians. Prior to this connection, the Grand Trunk ran from Montreal to Portland, by-passing Lewiston. New sources of rural labor in northern Maine and Quebec were now available to Lewiston's mill recruiting agents. Driven by depleted farmlands, poverty and a lack of local economic opportunities, rural inhabitants of these areas sought work in the expanding mill industries. Newspapers in both Maine and Massachusetts carried advertisements touting the desirability of wage labor work in the Lewiston mills.[16] The size of Lewiston's population and its direct railroad connection to Quebec were highly attractive to French Canadians, in comparison to the larger and more distant Southern New England industries.

In addition to industry's organized recruitment campaigns, the close kinship network of French Canadians facilitated transnational communication and the awareness of economic opportunity for their friends and relative in Lewiston. Thus, the combination of affordable and direct rail travel, intra-familiar communication and the relative geographical proximity of Lewiston drew rural French Canadian laborers into the mills. The first immigrants were from Quebec and were followed by Acadians from the Maritime Provinces and the St. John River Valley.[17]

The Franklin Company began to divest its monopoly on water-power rights to the Androscoggin River through the sale of 1,400 of its 4,000 shares to the Union Water Power Company in the early 1890s. By 1899 the Franklin Company would sell the remaining shares after much "protracted wrangling with the city of Lewiston over private control of the City's water supply."[18] This restructuring allowed the Franklin Company to evolve into a land management firm that leased lots to investors and individual property owners to construct their own concerns on these sites. Individual French Canadian families who desired dwellings in Lewiston's developing French Canadian neighborhoods, Petit Canada, sought out local financing negotiated by the Franklin Company. The arrangements benefited the Franklin Company stockholders while providing basic housing in a familiar environment to the uprooted.

By the latter part of the nineteenth century the city of Lewiston had become particularly attractive to both industrialists and an immigrant work force. The geographic location of Lewiston in central Maine was specifically desirable to the migrating French Canadian immigrants who were anxious to find wage labor in the New England textile mills. Lewiston was closer to Quebec both geographically and in travel time (due to the

Grand Trunk Railroad) in comparison to similar urban textile centers located in New England, such as the mills in Manchester, New Hampshire; Woonsocket, Rhode Island; and, Lowell, Lawrence, and Fall River, Massachusetts.[19]

By 1900 Lewiston was the second most populous city in Southern Maine, only exceeded by the former capital city of Portland. Lewiston, and its smaller twin city Auburn, contained nearly 15 percent of Maine's population in 1900, as shown by the U.S. Census figures for that year. Lewiston's French Canadian immigrants had grouped themselves in an ethnically and geographically defined space, known as Petit Canada. Within these segregated neighborhoods French Canadians became separated from the dominant Yankee culture through a network of formalized social structures which lessened their need for support from their host environment. As one historian observed, the formation of a Petit Canada neighborhood provided the French Canadian inhabitants with "emotional sustenance, psychological security, and a sense of meaning."[20] A consequence of this separatism was it protected and nurtured the identity and religiosity of the migrating French Canadians who were living in the shadows of their New England Yankee-dominated mill towns. Lewiston's own Petit Canada was a geographically bounded area that was defined by a community of tightly packed three to four story tenements built between the streets of Oxford, Lincoln, Cedar and Chestnut. This created a rectangular district also sometimes identified by the inhabitants as "the Island." The real estate that comprised this zone, prior to its development had been specifically designated by the directors of the Franklin Company for development by the French Canadian work force as it would locate their homes in close proximity to the mills.

This geographical separatism allowed the first inhabitants of Petit Canada to be left alone to follow the praxis of their own French Canadian culture with minimal social conflict from the city's Protestant and Anglophone Catholic communities. The apparent benign neglect of their established and defined immigrant community by the host environment encouraged the leaders of Petit Canada to assume that the establishment of an order of women religious from their Quebecois culture would be met with little negativity by city authorities. As this community of women religious would live and primarily minister within the boundaries of Lewiston's Petit Canada, their ethnic environment would also isolate them from Yankee bigotry. Yet, while the geographical isolation of Petit Canada nurtured a separatist mentality among the inhabitants which allowed them to sustain their cultural identity, it nevertheless also slowly fed a fundamental Yankee distrust of people who did not participate in their shared communal values and activities. This distrust was fueled as the French Canadians

began to build institutions that structurally maintained, and even empow-
ered, their cultural separatism.

   The contemporary idea of cultural diversity as a sociologically posi-
tive contribution to the American culture was not a valued belief in nineteenth-century Yankee society. Immigrants, especially if they were poor,
illiterate, and Catholic, were minimally tolerated as long as they remained
docile and invisible to their better educated and financed Protestant coun-
trymen. Yet the demographical dynamics of the Catholic immigrant migration to industrializing nineteenth-century Protestant America prevented
invisibility and subservience. It has been calculated that by 1860, the
Catholic population in America had reached 3,303,000, a 97 percent
increase in thirty years. As with Lewiston's French Canadians, the majority
of these immigrant Catholics were not Anglo-Saxon English-speaking
immigrants, but were Irish, German, French, Italian and Polish.[21] It was
simply numerically impossible for the American host culture to fully absorb
and assimilate this population into a Yankee defined cultural matrix that
eliminated all ethnic and religious distinctions.

   To establish the precise numbers of French Canadian as a subgroup that
belong to the mass immigrant migration to the United States prior to 1890 is
statistically problematic.[22] There is, nevertheless, one analysis that argues to
the contrary and attempts to provide precise population calculations of
French Canadians living in Maine. According to this research, in 1860 there
were 7,490 French Canadians living in the state. Twenty years later this population had expanded to 29,000 French Canadians. By the turn of the century
77,000 French Canadians were recorded as Maine inhabitants with the largest
concentration in the Northern counties.[23] This research remains controversial.
Yves Roby has estimated the combined population of French Canadians for
Lewiston and Auburn in the nineteenth century. According to Roby's estimate, in 1880 there were 4,714 French Canadians worshiping in Lewiston
and Auburn. By the turn of the century this population had expanded to
13,300 adherents.[24] Using parish records from the national French Canadian
parish in Lewiston, another estimate of French Canadian population can be
made, with an estimated 5,233 attending Saint Pierre in 1889 and 12,546 in
1900.[25] Figure 7 illustrates the trend line growth from 1870 to 1910 of French
Canadian population in Lewiston and Auburn, as measured by the growth in
attendance at the national parish of Saint Pierre; compared to the total population growth in Lewiston over the same period. Even using the most conser-
vative estimates, the growth rate of parish attendees was typically greater than
that for Lewiston as a whole during most of this time, meaning that the net
population growth of Lewiston at this time was largely French Canadian,
especially between 1880 and 1900.

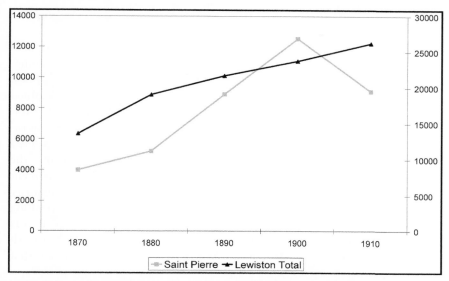

Figure 7: Lewiston and Saint Pierre Growth of Population, 1870–1910.

The explosive rate of the Catholic French Canadian population growth stretched the resources of the national parish of Saint Pierre to its limit. The Portland diocese responded by establishing two additional French Canadian national parishes in Lewiston and Auburn. Saint Louis parish was established across the river from Petit Canada in Auburn in 1902. Saint Mary's parish was formed within the heart of Petit Canada in 1907. The decline in population for Saint Pierre between 1900 and 1910 was due to the establishment of these churches, as their congregations would have most likely have attended Saint Pierre prior to their formation. The Saint Louis Church has continued to minister to the inhabitants of this parish to the present day. Saint Mary's Church was closed in 2002. The church facility was remodeled into a French Canadian cultural heritage museum in 2003.

Despite the lack of certainty regarding over the precise numerical size of the French Canadian migration to the state of Maine during the latter part of the nineteenth century, what is certain is that it was extensive and that it contributed to a fundamental alteration in the religious identity of the host culture. This in turn resulted in social upheaval that was accompanied by a pervasive cultural tension between Catholic adherents versus those who professed some form of Protestantism. As Maine's mill towns transformed from rural-based economies into industrial urban centers, this religious tension became both a source of bigotry as well as a source of altruism in both cultures.

Figure 2.1 Lewiston and Auburn French-Canadian Population, 1870–1930.

Chapter Four
Religious and Ethnic Struggles

THE IRISH

According to the records maintained in the Chancery of the Diocese of Portland, there was no accounting of Catholics living in Lewiston in 1846. Four years later, however, a congregation of 764 communicants spread among 125 Irish Catholic families was recorded by visiting priests.[1] The Irish first congregated in the area around Lincoln Street as it was walking distance to the mills, the canal, railways and their first chapel. The parish of Saint Joseph would be established by the Most Reverend Bishop David W. Bacon, Maine's first Catholic bishop, to serve this expanding community. The first chapel used by the parish was an abandoned Baptist facility located on Lincoln Street that had been purchased in 1855 by Reverend Peter McLaughlin.[2] This building was refurbished and became Saint John's Chapel.

The developing Catholic community was not viewed with favor by Lewiston's Protestant community. The combination of job competition and religious differences between the two groups fueled "bitter antagonism." Lewiston Yankees came to resent what they judged as "the invasion of the new faith" into their city. Yet their resentment towards the Irish did somewhat decrease as the English speaking Irish quickly assimilated into Lewiston's community of wage laborers.[3] A pervasive Yankee hostility towards Catholicism and its institutions, however, remained throughout the early decades of the twentieth century, often culminating in local Ku Klux Klan marches throughout Maine.

The first resident pastor to Saint Joseph's parish was Reverend John Cullen, 1857–1858. Prior to the founding of Saint Joseph, the spiritual needs of Lewiston's Catholic community were attended to by a series of visiting Irish Catholic priests from Portsmouth, New Hampshire, and

Portland, Bath, and Biddeford, Maine. These early clergy were: Charles McCallion (1850–1851); John O'Donnell (1851–1855); Peter McLaughlin (1855–1855); and Thomas Kennedy (1855–1857).[4] These priests celebrated Mass in Saint John's chapel, in private homes, as well as on industrial properties such as the Cowan Mill or in the Bates Dye-House. The recognition by Lewiston's local mill authorities of the importance of the Catholic Mass and a sacred place to worship among the Irish Catholic workers facilitated mutuality and cooperation between the two groups with management profiting. Yet, the majority of Lewiston's Protestant community that was not connected financially to the city's industrial community "resented" the "new faith" in their Yankee-controlled city.[5]

The dynamics of this situation were dramatically illustrated in the suspicious fire that severely damaged Saint John's Chapel in 1863. Local non-Catholics sabotaged rescue efforts while the onsite Franklin Company director, Albert Kelsey, labored to save the burning chapel. Years later, Kelsey spoke about the events of that night and subsequent developments in a newspaper interview. He referred to the local bigotry and "a sort of A.P.A-ism" that led to the act of arson.[6] He stated that hundreds of Lewiston residents turned out to jeer at the Catholics trying to fight the fire, and that someone had cut the fire engine's hose, so it was useless in fighting the flames. In dramatic fashion, Kelsey recalled how he had ordered the Bates Mill hose brought out and guards posted along its length; then before turning it on the flames that were engulfing the chapel, he turned the hose first on the shouting rabble and scattered them "like flies before a shower." However, the building was extensively damaged, rendering it unusable. Lewiston's fledging Catholic community was now homeless.

The burning of Saint John's Chapel was not an isolated incident of bigotry according to Kelsey. He remembered overt anti-Catholic bias by his employers following the fire, when the Reverend Peter McLaughlin requested that Lewiston's Catholics be treated as other Christian congregations in Lewiston and also be given a grant of land from the Franklin Company for the construction of a church. Kelsey presented McLaughlin's request to his board of directors in Boston and was surprised at the vehemence with which it was received by several directors who swore that Catholicism did not have a place in their developing industrial city. He then sent McLaughlin down to meet with the board, but the anti-Catholic members insulted and humiliated the priest at their meeting. This was the last straw for Kelsey. After hearing McLaughlin's recounting of his trip, Kelsey immediately offered him the best remaining lot in Lewiston for a Catholic church and gave it to him at a cut-rate price. He made sure that the deed, while in the name of the Portland Bishop, did not carry his title, so that it would be approved by the Franklin Company board. When criticized by the company president for his religious tolerance, Kelsey threatened to resign saying that: " . . . the right and wrong of the matter, the question as to whether you are justified in trying to keep the Catholic Church out of Lewiston, we will not discuss . . . [t]hat is all there is to say on the subject."[7] As a result of Kelsey's inclusive vision, a new Catholic church was to be built. Saint Joseph's Church was designed by Patrick C. Keely of New York and was completed by 1867 at the cost of $55,000.[8]

Despite strong suspicions among local Catholics that the fire of Saint John's Chapel was purposely set, the following years in Lewiston were a period of growth and stability for Saint Joseph's Catholic congregation; relatively devoid of more overt acts of bigotry. The cornerstone of Saint Joseph Church was laid by Bishop Bacon on June 13, 1864. The congregation celebrated their first Mass in the new church on April 14, 1867. Bishop Bacon, however, did not officially dedicate Saint Joseph until June 13, 1869.[9] This was an English-speaking Catholic community in an English-speaking Protestant society. The power of a common linguistic heritage to facilitate acceptance and assimilation was a significant cause in the subsequent treatment of Saint Joseph's Irish Catholics by Lewiston's Yankee host culture.

Over the following three decades Saint Joseph's parish flourished, as seen in Figure 8, growing more than 37 percent from 1877 to 1894. The expansion of the population strained the existing facility and under the

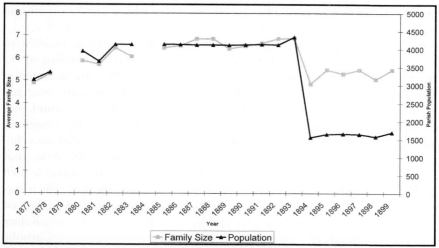

Figure 8: Saint Joseph Parish Population and Family Size, 1877-1900.

administration of Reverend Thomas Wallace plans were drawn to divide
the parish. The petition for division was submitted on October 29, 1894 to
Portland's Bishop the Most Reverend James A. Healy. In a letter to Wallace
approving the division dated March 16, 1895 Michael C. O'Brien, the
Vicar General for the Portland Diocese stated:

> "The former English-speaking Parish of St. Joseph is divided and made
> into two parishes, to [be] known as St. Joseph and St. Patrick's respec-
> tively. This division is to date from the second Sunday of November,
> A.D. 1894; the dividing line in Lewiston shall be Ash Street, the canal
> and Cross Street, but both sides of the streets mentioned shall belong to
> St. Joseph's Parish; and in Auburn the line will be the Grand Trunk
> Railway."[10]

This parish division is clearly seen in Figure 8, as the parish population
dropped from 4,334 to about 1,600 in 1895. Average family size dropped
as well, perhaps indicating that the older parish retained the older, more
established families. Saint Patrick's congregation was also composed predominantly of Irish and other Anglophone Catholics. The French Canadian
national parish, Saint Pierre was established in 1870, one year after Saint
Joseph and twenty-five years prior to Saint Patrick's.

Illustrating the dynamics of Lewiston's ethnic Catholic communities requires an analysis of their growth rate in comparison to the total
city population. A formal systematic accounting by the state of the
births, marriage, divorce and death rates among Maine inhabitants was
not initiated until 1892.[11] The city of Lewiston, which was incorporated
on March 5, 1863, only provided population statistics in the city's yearly
report. Catholic parishes in Lewiston did provide to the Diocese of Portland a yearly accounting of population size, numbers of families, marriages and baptisms of its congregation. These records were written by
the pastor and there are many apparent errors and omission in these
reports. There were two parish reports for the Saint Joseph community
representing the year 1877. Both reports were prepared by the pastor of
Saint Joseph, Reverend Thomas Wallace. Yet Wallace recorded two different totals for the population size of Saint Joseph in 1877. In one
record he recorded that the total Catholic population was "about 3000"
and in the other "about 3200." While this discrepancy must be
acknowledged, the data from the reports, even if possibly flawed, represents the best available data and can be used to construct general size
and growth trends of Lewiston's Catholic population with a reasonable
degree of certitude.

Due to the nature of these sources only gross population figures are used in the following analysis of Lewiston's ethnic Catholic communities in comparison to the total population growth of the city. Comparisons between Lewiston's different Catholic ethnic communities does however, include marriage and baptismal rates, which were drawn from the Diocese of Portland parish reports. This information provides a more complete picture of these communities which illustrates their differences.

THE FRENCH CANADIANS

The first documented Catholic French Canadians living in Lewiston were George Carignan and his family. According to documents in the Diocese of Portland Chancery Archives, Carignan arrived in Lewiston from Kingsey, Quebec in 1860. Lewiston's French Canadian newspaper *Le Messager* also supported Carignan's claim in an 1892 article. As previously acknowledged estimates of the size of the nineteenth-century immigration of French Canadians to the United States in general and to Lewiston in particular remain controversial. What can be surmised fairly accurately is that during the decades between 1850 and 1900 several hundred thousand migrating French Canadians became American immigrants.[12]

Ten years after George Carignan and his family had immigrated to Lewiston there was a relatively small community of approximately 689 French Canadians in the city. Like the Irish, the French Canadians first settled in the Lincoln Street area; and for similar reasons. As the Irish community expanded north and east into formerly Yankee neighborhoods, the French Canadians moved into their former tenement housing. The French Canadian community would continue to grow slowly at a steady pace. In 1880 this community was estimated to be 4,000 to 5,000.[13] The pace of immigration would dramatically increase during the 1880s and 1890s. In the late 1880s as many as sixty-five French Canadians were arriving in Lewiston per day. By 1895 this community would number over 10,000.[14]

The majority of French Canadians who migrated to New England in search of wage employment accepted harsh working conditions with minimal protest. In Lewiston the textile mills dominated the semi-skilled market and became the employer of most French Canadians. According to statistics compiled from the Lewiston textile industry during the last decades of the nineteenth century, 94 percent of working French Canadian women labored in the mills. They were joined by 42 percent of the working French Canadian men, and 96 percent of the working French Canadian children. 80 percent of all French Canadian households had at least one member employed in the textile mills with 31 percent of all households fully dependent upon that industry.[15] The employers of the French Canadians judged them to be "docile, industrial [and] averse to unions."[16] Non-mill employment was secured in either a semi-skilled occupation or by working in a small family-owned business.

The employment of French Canadian children in Lewiston's mills was necessary for the economic survival of their families and was allowed under Maine law. The United States Congress did not outlaw child labor until 1916 and only regulated businesses engaged in foreign and interstate commerce. The law stipulated that children had to be fourteen years of age in order to work in mills and industrial factories. The work week was limited to six days, with 7:00 P.M. mandated as the end of the work day.[17]

The employment pattern of Maine's French Canadians was reflected in the *Eleventh Census of the United States, 1890*. This was the first census to include some statistics on French Canadians as a separate ethnicity. The three major occupations for Canadian-born French men in 1890 after the textile industry were: non-specific laborers, farmers, and saw and plane mill employees. For Canadian-born French women the three most common occupations other than employment in the textile industry were: domestic servant, garment trade worker, and shoe factory worker.[18]

French Canadians who immigrated to Maine thus occupied the bottom strata of the state's social-economic system. In addition they also faced religious segregation and derogatory treatment from the established community of Irish Anglophone Catholics, especially as their population expanded. This antagonism towards the French Canadian by the Irish was greater than the Irish dislike of Lewiston's Yankees.[19] Lewiston's French Canadians thus lived on the margin of an Anglophone-controlled society that contributed to their segregation within their neighborhood, Petit Canada. Their Catholic coreligionists, the Irish community of Saint Joseph parish comfortably established in their new church on Main Street, did not aggressively integrate their Francophone brethren into their faith community.[20]

Records from the Portland Chancery claim that there were an estimated 1,000 French Canadians worshiping at Saint Joseph's Church by 1869. If they chose to pray in the main church, the clergy did not encourage liturgies to be held in their native language. Instead these French speaking Catholics were relegated to the basement, where their spiritual needs were ministered in the French language by the Flemish associate pastor Abbe Louis Mutsaers (1868–1870). The religious friction between theses immigrant coreligionists has been historically credited as "one of the great stimul[i] to the foundation of French parishes in New England." This Irish-French antagonism led one French Canadian priest to ponder "whether God was going to separate" the Irish and the French Canadians in heaven.[21]

The expansion of the French-Canadian community, the unique structure of their ethnic socio-religious culture, and the above described ethnic disharmony forced Portland's Bishop David Bacon to establish a separate French parish for the Lewiston community in 1870. Saint Pierre was the first French national parish in the Portland Diocese and the eleventh in New England.[22] The bishop then had to find a French-speaking priest to serve the newly formed Lewiston congregation. This decision required the bishop to make an open appeal to the French-speaking Catholic community throughout the United States and Canada. An answer to Bacon's appeal was received from Reverend Edouard Letourneau who arrived from Saint-Hyacinthe, Quebec in 1870.[23]

While Letourneau only served as a priest to the Lewiston French Canadian community for one year, he successfully obtained the loan of the small chapel of Saint John on Lincoln Street for his congregation. This was the same chapel that was suspiciously burnt in 1863. Following the fire, repairs had been made to the building so it could once again serve as a house of worship. Within the walls of this tiny chapel, Letourneau celebrated the first mass for Lewiston's Saint Pierre community on July 2, 1870.

After services, these immigrant worshippers could step outside and see two structures that intimately comprised their new world. One was the Bates Mill complex and the other was the Grand Trunk Railroad station. These two structures, along with their church, would become the matrix that sustained the wealth, the familiar religiosity and the heritage of Lewiston's French Canadian immigrant community as it transitioned over the decades into its new American industrial environment. The mills were their place of work, the parish was their place of faith, family and fellowship, and the Grand Truck Railroad was the means to their past, which ironically, was also the vehicle that had transported them into their future and eventual assimilation into the American culture.

When Letourneau left the parish of Saint Pierre, he was replaced by Reverend Pierre Hevey, a native of Saint-Hyacinthe, Quebec. It is argued that the credit of being called the "founding pastor" of Saint Pierre's parish should be awarded to Hevey not Letourneau.[24] This argument is based upon the evidence drawn from Hevey's ten-year reign as the spiritual leader to Lewiston's French Canadians, which tenure gave him the authority not only to direct the community's growth, but the time to let his entrepreneurial abilities successfully operate and expand his domain and that of his congregation.

Five months after Hevey became the pastor to the French-Canadian congregation worshiping at the little chapel of Saint John, he successfully petitioned Bishop Bacon to grant him permission to form a savings enterprise that would pay for the construction of a new and larger church for his parish. Hevey devised a self-financing plan whereby parish members deposited funds at a saving bank and received a small interest payment on the principal. The first depositor was Eleusippe Garneau for the amount of ten dollars. Nine years later the bank would have assets of $100,000. While this financial enterprise dissolved when Hevey was transferred to Manchester, New Hampshire in 1881, he used the self-funding concept in his new parish and founded the first credit union in the United States, Sainte-Marie in Manchester.[25]

The combination of Hevey's business acumen and aggressive real estate search in Lewiston culminated in the acquisition of property on Bartlett Street for the founding of Saint Pierre Church. On July 7, 1872, Bishop Bacon blessed and laid the cornerstone for the new brick church, which was quickly opened for services in the autumn of 1872. Saint Pierre Church was officially dedicated on May 4, 1873. The local newspaper would comment on the occasion that it was "a strange and suggestive sight! These 2,000 French people consecrating a church worth $50,000 after living here only 3 years in a foreign land and before they have homes of their own."[26] In 2005 the church of Saint Pierre, now known as Saints Peter and Paul, was made a minor Basilica, recognizing its cultural importance and its magnificence as the second-largest Catholic church in New England.

Surviving parish records place the cost of the property, building materials, furnishings and the organ at approximately $100,000. Saint Pierre Church was composed of over 60,000 red bricks, was 116 feet long, 32 feet wide and had a 160 foot high bell tower. The French Canadian congregation that accomplished this feat was comprised of 2,054 immigrant and first generation French Canadians. As seen in Figure 9, the parish would expand to 2,604 during the next year and would grow to almost 8,400 by 1900. Interestingly, the average family size at this parish, dropped from near seven down to five over the twenty-five years from 1876 to 1900. This may be attributed to a continued influx of workers who were either unmarried or left their family behind. A high child mortality rate during the early years of this community also diminished family numbers. One such tragic birthing history is provided later in the chapter. A final possibility was that as French Canadians gained a more secure economic status in Lewiston's business community and labor markets, a large family composed of two parents, many children and often hosting one or more single relatives, was no longer economically necessary. By comparison, as shown in Figure 8, the more "settled"

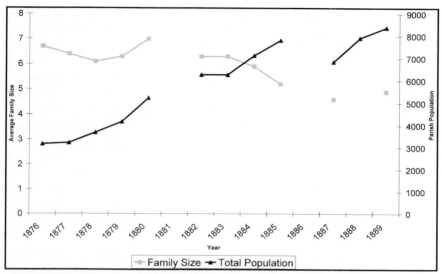

Figure 9: Saint Pierre Parish Population and Family Size, 1876–1890.

parish of Saint Joseph showed a steady increase in family size from about five in 1877 to a peak of seven in 1893, immediately before the parish division of 1894.

Yet as the majority of Petit Canada's residents remained wage laborers, they were financially dependent upon market conditions within the textile industry and the whim of the mill overseer. This, in turn, contributed to economic insecurity in the French Canadian community, with harsh consequences when unemployment occurred or if wages were docked for unsatisfactory work. Scribbled on the top of a payroll ledger from the Libby Mill was the following note: "pieces which were reported as having ends on salvage" and "as these p[ie]ces are on payment ending Apr[il] 4th you will take this fine out of their [the weavers] wages due Saturday April 11- 08."[27] The combination of job and wage insecurity, coupled with Lewiston's limited social welfare resources, meant that unemployment or missed wages could quickly lead to poverty and starvation for the inhabitants of Petit Canada.

French Canadian immigrants throughout New England responded to the marginalization caused by such economic conditions by constructing a complex network of mutual aid societies. These organizations were a matrix of social support, economic assistance and welfare aid. In Lewiston the French Canadians practiced a communal welfare strategy centered on a kin network system that was facilitated by their parish of Saint Pierre. It was not until the arrival of the Grey Nuns in 1878 that any structured social welfare system began to emerge that recognized and directed specific resources to mitigate the poverty and illiteracy of the French Canadians who worked in Lewiston's textile mills.

The social segregation, impoverishment, and economic uncertainty of the French Canadian community of wage-laborers thus forced the community to turn inward and search within the resources of its immigrant society for benevolence. Under Hevey's leadership, a Lewiston chapter of a fraternal organization, the Saint-Jean-Baptiste Society, was established in 1872. The purpose of this society, in addition to professing a moral agenda and religious goals, was to provide mutual aid benefits to those French Canadians in need and to fight for "the preservation of national character and faith."[28] By 1875, the Lewiston chapter of the Saint-Jean-Baptiste Society would be subsumed into another French Canadian fraternal organization, the Institut Jacques-Cartier.[29]

The economic and social marginization of the French Canadians also fostered communal anxiety when the inhabitants of Petit Canada encountered the physical truths shared by all humanity regardless of social status or class: birth, illness, and death. While the French Canadian fraternal organizations did provide minimal economic assistance in times of illness and death, their resources were inadequate when confronted by the welfare and medical needs of their community.

A brief account of the life of one French Canadian woman provides a haunting insight into the tragic realities of poverty, illness and death that too often defined an immigrant's world in nineteenth-century Lewiston. Virginia Deshayes Dutille was a French Canadian, Catholic, married and a member of Saint Pierre's parish. On February 16, 1877 she gave birth to a son, Louis Arthur, who lived for thirteen days. Ten months later Virginia gave birth to a daughter, Lumina Exila. Lumina lived one more day than her older brother Louis dying on December 20, 1877. In one year Virginia had borne and buried two children. Four years later she gave birth to another son Jean Thomas on March 15, 1882. Jean lived for three weeks, seven more days than Lumina, dying on April 3, 1882. Two years would elapse before Virginia had another child. Her daughter Anne was born on August 9, 1884, surviving a single day. Ten months later, another daughter, Alphonsine Emelda, was born on June 23, 1885. Alphonsine thrived for eight months but could not survive a Maine winter. She died on February 23, 1886. Virginia's last daughter Aime Angelique was born on July 1889 and lived two years; not dying until the spring of 1892. Fifteen months after Aime's death Virginia's husband Louis died on July 1, 1893. At the time of his death Louis was forty years old and Virginia was a thirty-nine year old widow. Virginia, however, was not alone. Necrology records indicate that one child of their union survived into adulthood. Their daughter Evelina was born in 1879, and did not succumb to death until January 24, 1902 at the age of twenty-three. Virginia lived for fourteen more years until her own death on May 8, 1916 at the age of sixty-two. In the six decades of her life Virginia had buried seven children and a husband.[30]

Of these seven children, only Evelina Dutille would have had the opportunity to receive an education that might have increased her employment options and ability to survive. Yet the lack of English among the French Canadians prevented their children from taking advantage of educational opportunities provided in Lewiston's schools. Language issues however were not the only deterrent to the French Canadian children attending Lewiston schools. The use of the Protestant Bible in the school curriculum was unacceptable and offensive to devout French Canadians who had endured the atrocities of England's ethnic cleansing of the Acadians. Such bitter memories ensured that French Canadian identity would be inextricably linked, through Catholic education, to the Catholic faith. A solution had to be found to resolve the twin demands of Lewiston's French Canadian immigrants for Catholic education and adequate health care.

In the next chapter, Lewiston's benevolence community and its relationship to the evolution of professional health care in hospital facilities in the United States will be explored. The issue behind the failure of these institutions to provide health and welfare care to the French Canadian immigrants is also examined. This information is vital to understanding why the Grey Nuns decided to build a system of hospital and welfare foundations in Lewiston. This material also clarifies why the Grey Nuns approached medical care and the establishment of their hospital as independent health care providers.

Chapter Five
Yankee Benevolence

As Lewiston transitioned from a rural township into an urban industrialized city, a minimalist theory towards charitable aid was adopted by civic authorities. This was especially evident in the fact that there was not a Poor Department established and funded by the city of Lewiston until April 1879, almost two decades after the town's municipal incorporation.[1]

Grounded in the traditions of Yankee class consciousness, Lewiston's elite interpreted dependency and disease as a reflection of personal failure. The conditions of illness and poverty were not interpreted as resulting from either environmental causalities or social victimization. This moralistic perspective contributed to a preference by Lewiston's elite for primitive institutional care facilities to address the city's obligation to those requiring aid. These institutions were the alms house, the city farm and the pest house. The city farm was founded on March 21, 1839. The alms house was established sometime prior to 1864. The pest house was never a permanent facility and was used when an epidemic occurred. It was abandoned once the contagion had been eradicated. Maine state law required that if an overseer of the poor was not elected at the town meeting a selectman would automatically serve as the overseer, which was the common practice adopted in Lewiston beginning in 1801.[2] Such a restrictive and judgmental approach towards aid, coupled with how benefits were allocated, impeded the establishment of a professional structured medical facility that practiced benevolent care in Lewiston. In the absence of professional medical and benevolent care, the physical and mental suffering endured by the poorer inhabitants of Lewiston became the cry of want. This situation was not effectively addressed until 1888 when the first health care facility was established by the Grey Nuns. They named their hospital Our Lady of Lourdes Asylum, but it was also commonly known as The Sisters' Hospital, and Saint-Hyacinthe Hospital.

Woven into the management of Lewiston's benevolence was a Protestant ethic grounded in the ideals of Christian stewardship, which directed benefits to those deemed worthy. Beginning in 1795 until its municipal incorporation in 1863, the town selectmen of Lewiston used a variety of aid programs in their "search for order," prior to deciding on institutionalization.[3] This resulted in a form of elite-bestowed benevolence, which dictated a culture of care that often ignored the humanity of the aid recipient.

The various provisions of aid programs which Lewiston adopted were detailed in the town records between 1795 and 1863. These programs included direct economic and material aid to the poor. Initially Lewiston pressured the relatives of dependents to ensure for their care or auctioned dependents to the highest bidder. Somewhat later, Lewiston's Overseer of the Poor undertook to provide minimal care and aid to the dependent and ill. Lewiston would also demand aid payments from another town if it could be proven that the person making the request for aid was originally a member of that township. The incarceration of the poor in a town-owned and operated benevolent facility ultimately emerged as the preferred method of providing aid.[4]

Lewiston's public auctions of the poor, 1822–1835, were grimly similar to a cattle auction. The poor were auctioned off at the town meeting to the lowest bidder. In the 1833 auction, the winning bidder was responsible for covering the expenses of the poor for board, clothing and nursing. The bidder was not responsible for medical and funeral expenses. Furthermore, if the poor were returned by their host they were to be "as well clad as when taken."[5] In exchange for their bid fee and responsibilities the bidder had the right to the labor of the poor. It was not uncommon for families to be split-up at these auctions and there was little sensitivity among the bidders for the special needs of the elderly or the infirm.[6] The bitter historical irony of these auctions is that today the state of Maine prides itself on its anti-slavery heritage as the home to Harriet Beecher Stowe and several stops on the Underground Railroad. While a public auction of the poor might seem extreme to our modern sensibility, it was only one part of a broader objective by the elite to maintain their authority to control both sum and substance of any aid as well as the selection of the deserving poor.

As Lewiston transitioned into a viable urban industrial center, institutionalization evolved as the preferred method of administering aid. If the diseased and degenerate lacked private resources and consequently were faced with starvation or death, they were incarcerated in the alms house and/or the city farm. During times of epidemics, the suffering poor could also be sent to the local pest house to isolate the spread of the contagion. The pest house was only used intermittently as a health care facility by Lewiston's civic authorities, usually during small pox epidemics. For example, the pest house was used in the 1900 and 1905 smallpox epidemics to house those stricken. The building was located on the outskirts of Lewiston, next to the Catholic Cemetery of Mount Hope. As one historian has insightfully observed, within these institutions, "the welfare of the patient was often secondary to the well-being of the society that required his isolation."[7]

Lewiston's city farm was a working-farm located on the outskirts of Lewiston where those poor deemed worthy were institutionalized if they fell into dependency.[8] An overseer supervised the farm inmates, the facility's budget, and the farm's production. The Lewiston alms house was the recipient of the indigent and the diseased. The Lewiston City Physician wrote the following report on his duties and opinion of Lewiston's alms house in the city's first annual report:

"Lewiston, March 10, 1864

To the Honorable City Council of Lewiston:

Gentlemen: My report as City Physician, I am happy to say is short. There have been but one death among the city paupers in the past year. Charles Palmer, aged four years, died at the Alms House, December 21, 1863, of tuberculosis. There have been five cases of alarm of small-pox within the past year, which I immediately reported to the Mayor, and such precautions were taken in each case, that it did not spread in a single instance.

I take the liberty here to make a few remarks about the inmates of the Alms House, although I may be transcending my duty. There are at the present time, twenty-five paupers at the Alms House; ten adults and fifteen children, a less number of children than usual. They occupy a room thirteen by fourteen feet as a sitting room. I think the sun never shines into the room, and it is poorly ventilated. The children are allowed to mingle with the adults, some of whom are so filthy and low as to be unfit companions for even the dregs of society. The language that the poor degraded creatures use, is no more proper for the children to hear, than the foul air that is poisoned by the filthy exhalations of the worst diseases, is proper for them to breath. Yet they are permitted to hear profane and obscene talk, and to breathe the foulest air. The evil should be immediately remedied by dividing them into wards, and a Matron employed to instruct and superintend the children.

Respectfully submitted by

Pearl Martin, City Physician."[9]

For Lewiston's suffering poor, the alms house was their last option before surrendering to their mortality. An urban alms house was typically a squalid facility that functioned to "demoralize its recipients" according to the medical historian Charles E. Rosenberg.[10] Neither the almshouse nor the city farm were institutions that followed the tenets of altruistic care. Both institutions were publicly supported by local taxes and responsible to politically elected authority.[11] The unfortunate who found themselves incarcerated in either institution were often judged by the local elite as belonging to the class of paupers or the undeserving poor, even when they were children.

When contextualized within the larger spectrum of the evolution of American social welfare policies, Lewiston's aid provisions were unfortunately not atypical. This lack of uniqueness does not render these practices anymore humane. An acute example of this behavior towards the poor was specifically demonstrated by the policy towards pauper children. These children were either bound-out or yearly, rented at public auction or, as in the fate of young Charles Palmer, abandoned to die at the alms house. Were the elite of Lewiston attempting to regulate the behavior of the poor or find a remedy to a crisis which they lacked economic and social resources to remedy? Rosenberg, Vogel, Dolan, Gilbert and other scholars have all argued that it was cultural, not economic factors that guided the provision of aid by the social and religious elite.[12] As Rosenberg wrote, "Pauperism was a central concept in the social understanding of these generations; it implied a moral bankruptcy, habitual willingness to accept charity in preference to working."[13] When the poor in Lewiston were stricken with smallpox, one wonders how gainful employment could have been maintained.

The Lewiston elite placed greater value on social and religious norms in the administration of aid than on economic factors. They masked their socio-religious agenda in convoluted public statements that juxtaposed contrary economic truths. In the annual report for 1878 the Overseer of the Poor exported the poor from Lewiston despite the "large" cost. The Overseer's decision was based upon the calculation that, in the long term, expulsion was the "cheapest" method when he wrote: "The large numbers of tramps that have called for assistance, have, in most every case, been sent away from the city. We deem this the most judicious and economical plan of dealing with this class, and while the cost in fares, &c., is quite large, yet in the end, it is the cheapest."[14]

Twelve years later E.F. Scuton, then Clerk for the Overseer of the Poor, would again reiterate this pernicious philosophy towards poverty and the provision of aid to the poor whom he identified as tramps:

"This is a class of people which is steadily on the increase. They are quite often taken sick on their arrival in our city, and we are obliged to furnish them medical assistance and support them until they are well. They are a menace to the lives and property of the citizens of any city or town through which they pass in their wanderings, and will always continue to be until laws are enacted to imprison them at hard labor wherever they are found, and are known by the authorities to be confirmed tramps."[15]

As these testimonies reveal, Lewiston's civic leaders believed that poverty was connected to personal failure whether physical, mental, or moral. In other words, the elite relegated those who endured personal failure, physical disability and dependency to a virtual criminal status. This belief was cemented to an understanding that if someone fell into a state of dependency, regardless of reasons, they constituted a local "menace" to the established population. As a group, this menace was a class of "confirmed tramps" that required either incarceration or removal. Such an understanding of illness and poverty justified, to the satisfaction of Lewiston's elites, the adoption of aid provision policies that negated their responsibility to provide benevolent long-term medical care to the poor.

In addition to the moralistic attitude held towards poverty by Lewiston's civic authorities, they also believed that acceptance of material support justified, if not obligated, surrendering of the recipient's personal freedom. Charles E. Rosenberg claims that: "Few who entered the almshouse did so voluntarily; it was the last resort for the city's most helpless and deprived."[16] Once incarcerated in the almshouse or city farm the poor became "inmates" who required strict environmental controls to regain morality, health, and perhaps even self-sufficiency. The acceptance of charity simultaneously led to the acceptance of imprisonment.

A CRY OF WANT

Influenced by Lewiston's emerging economic status, the Maine State Fair was relocated to Lewiston in 1870. Among the Fair's diverse attractions that year were the birth of a child in a horse stall and the death of a man in the Lewiston Common Council room. Local newspapers reported that the man's death could have been avoided and perhaps a better birth site could have been found if Lewiston had a "suitable place" for medical care.[17]

As previously examined, there were two established city supported institutions in Lewiston that were dedicated to allocating long-term benefits to aid the dependent and the ill: the city farm and the alms house. Both of these institutions also functioned as reform facilities. Medical care services statewide were also limited. There were only three hospitals formally recognized by the American Medical Association in the entire state: the Maine Insane Hospital located in Augusta, founded in 1835; the U.S. Marine Hospital, Portland, founded in 1856; and the Maine General Hospital, in Portland, founded in 1871.[18]

As Lewiston underwent industrialization and urbanization, the percent of the population that lived in poverty dramatically expanded. In 1864, the Report of the City Auditor recorded an expenditure of $3987.75 for the poor. This figure included the building supplies for the alms house.[19] Six years later the Annual City Report recorded $5101.80 spent for the support of the poor and $3904.52 for maintaining the city farm and alms house.[20] When the Grey Nuns arrived in Lewiston in 1878, the expenditure for support of the poor had increased almost 300 percent to $17,750.28 while only $4,098.15 went for maintaining the city farm, yet this was only two percent of the City's total budget of $730,798.55.[21]

Despite the expansion of Lewiston's support to the poor, the recipients of aid could no longer be classified as paupers by the late nineteenth century. Lewiston's poor had evolved into a socio-economic class that encompassed members of a wage-labor class who had migrated to Lewiston in search of employment in the textile mills and not in search of institutional incarceration. The wage-labor class evolved into a proletariat that could not be classified as the unworthy poor or mere tramps. Rather they became the class of worthy poor whose labors underpinned the city's economic expansion.

The perception of poverty by Lewiston's civic leaders did evolve. Levi Greenleaf, the clerk and agent of Lewiston's Overseer of the Poor admitted by 1893 that: "We have undoubtedly made some errors in judgment in dealing with the hundreds who have sought aid from the city, but we have endeavored to do our duty and if to err at all, to do so on the side of humanity."[22] Greenleaf called for a change in Lewiston's aid to the poor, but in language which still maintained the rhetoric of nineteenth-century paternalism:

> "We believe it to be in the interest of good government, of the future and the rising generation, to *be good to the poor*" to aid them in every proper way to be good citizens and gain the influences and advantages of our public institutions; to bring them up out of poverty and low dens of filth and ignorance into the light of day, thus sending new hopes and gladness into their hearts, enabling them to over-ride obstacles and finally becoming not only self-supporting but good thrifty people."[23]

Greenleaf's altruism, however, was not extended to immigrants who settled in Lewiston in search of wage labor but instead found only unemployment. For these unfortunate, Greenleaf still voiced the exportation solution to mitigate unemployment: "Quite a large number of people who have become unable to work and who have been residents in the city but a short time, have been sent to Canada and other places from whence they came."[24] It must be acknowledged that Greenleaf's report was written during the advent of the second-worst economic depression experienced in American history. This may explain his somewhat compassionate stance towards recognizing Lewiston's obligation to its native poor on one hand versus providing benefits to a group of unemployed immigrants on the other. Furthermore, in light of the emerging social welfare network that operated within Lewiston's French Canadian community, one can presume that those who were returned to Quebec lived on the margin of the Lewiston settlement and lacked family support, or a firm connection to the community.

In addition to the absence of humane civic welfare institutions, Lewiston's expanding French Canadian immigrant proletariat was vulnerable to a myriad of abuses ranging from bigotry to unsafe environmental standards in their residences and places of work.[25] Such unsafe conditions were not of workers' making and were beyond their ability to control. Lewiston's mayor William H. Newell openly acknowledged this situation in the city's Health Department Report: "It must not be forgotten that the death rate in Lewiston is very high, and that portions of Lewiston are thickly settled."[26] The payroll ledgers of Lewiston's Libby textile mills contain notes pertaining to workers' absenteeism and illnesses. Whatever air was available within the confines of a textile mill was heavily laden with organic material from the cotton that was being processed into fabric. Furthermore the noise generated from the looms was deafening. The effects of this polluted atmosphere upon the mill workers was severe and eventually would lead the Grey Nuns to establish an out-patient clinic dedicated to treating complaints of the eyes, ears and throat. Overseers, as noted previously, took pay deductions from worker's pay if any imperfections were found on the fabric. Such penalties were imposed regardless if the damage to the fabric was the result of weaver error and according to surviving documents the majority of fines were extracted from the earnings of female weavers. The worker had no avenue for disputing any fines. Effective collective bargaining by the employees and the rights of women labor remained in the industry's future. It must be recognized, however, that French Canadian mill workers' own mild conduct led mill management to prefer them over other ethnicities "primarily because they were viewed as docile pawns to be manipulated in [their] struggle with trade unionism."[27] This attitude towards the French Canadian worker was so common that in 1882, the head of the Massachusetts Bureau of Statistics of Labor wrote that employers "prefer them [French Canadians] in their mills; for they are industrious in the extreme, do not grumble about pay, are docile, and have nothing to do with labor agitations."[28] Finally, as the great majority of recorded fines were levied against female workers by male overseers, such as in the Libby Mill, the reality of sexual discrimination, if not abuse, must be acknowledged.[29] The illnesses, fines, abuse, and harsh environmental conditions which Lewiston's proletariat endured provide ample testimony to the critical need for the establishment of structured benevolent and medical care facilities focused upon the needs of the poor and wage laborers.

Sending the working poor to either the alms house or the city farm by the late nineteenth century was not only inappropriate, but also logistically and financially impossible due to the size of the wage-labor class. The elite realized that a remedy to this situation was urgent if the spread of poverty was to be halted before it found a more militant or politically active solution. Unionization and socialism were unacceptable to the nineteenth-century secular and religious authorities; fear of such became an underlying motivating force in the creation of social welfare resources for the poor. Motivated by varying proportions of economic self-interest and genuine idealism, Lewiston's political and religious leaders began to draw support from local philanthropists for establishment of additional social welfare institutions in the last decades of the twentieth century.

Prior to the arrival of the Grey Nuns, medical care in Lewiston was class based and selective. A few health care professionals, under the leadership of Bates and Harvard educated Edward H. Hill, had created the Androscoggin County Medical Association (ACMA) in the 1860s. The primary objective of the ACMA, however, was not to provide medical aid to Lewiston's wage-laborers and immigrant community. Rather the ACMA sought to establish a hospital structured in accordance with Protestant benevolence and securely funded by city, state and private sources which took several years to achieve. The acquisition of the financial resources required to establish the ACMA hospital will be discussed in the following chapter. But it must be mentioned that a critically unfortunate consequence of the ACMA fundraising agenda was that the acute medical needs of the working class, specifically French Canadian immigrants, were slighted during their fundraising efforts.

In conclusion, a fundamental principle in Lewiston's practice of benevolence and medical care during the latter part of the nineteenth century stressed both a punitive and paternal, rather than an altruistic approach, towards illness and dependency. This directly contributed to the absence of compassionate, affordable, long-term medical care that was directed towards the needs of the wage-labor class and immigrant communities. By the time the Grey Nuns arrived in Lewiston in 1878, the elite had encoded their understanding of aid into the city's political culture. Even so, as acknowledged by Levi Greenleaf, this poor and culturally marginalized population was perhaps morally deserving of aid, if it was employed or employable.

Chapter Six
First Foundations

"AN ORPHANAGE WITH HOSPITAL WINGS"

By 1888 two separate and distinct hospitals were simultaneously emerging in Lewiston. One was under the authority of the Androscoggin County Medical Association, (ACMA), and it was moneyed, privileged, Protestant and male. The other hospital, the Asylum of Our Lady of Lourdes was poor, immigrant, Catholic and female. Between 1885 to 1888, the Grey Nuns recorded providing care for thirty-six women and children.[1] The ACMA could not make a similar claim, since their hospital was still only theoretical. Due to a fundraising dilemma, the ACMA's ability to proceed with the establishment of a permanent hospital facility had been compromised.[2] The ACMA did, however, draw up incorporation papers for their hospital on December 26, 1888, calling it Central Maine General Hospital. But it was not until the Central Maine General Hospital board secured $10,000 in a State grant matched by public donations, that the Bearce Estate, in Lewiston was purchased and then renovated into a hospital. Once construction was completed, Central Maine General Hospital admitted its first patient, eighteen-year-old Charles Teague, on July 2, 1891.[3] By this time, the Grey Nuns had been caring for Lewiston's poor for ten years and had been providing comprehensive medical care for three.

The Grey Nun leadership and the trustees of the ACMA both experienced the difficulties of foundation building for the purpose of establishing a hospital. Unlike the ACMA, the Grey Nuns' situation was critical, for they were already providing medical services. While the lack of funds had stopped the ACMA from establishing a hospital on anything more than paper, the Grey Nuns had actively engaged as sister-nurses since their arrival in 1878 regardless of financial obstacles. Neither the absence of a medical facility or a secure source of funding deterred the sisters from ministering care. Neither did the additional responsibilities of educating Petit Canada's children. Drawing from their religious training and practices, the sisters interpreted difficulties and obstacles as an opportunity to live in closer union with the suffering Christ of their faith. The founding stories of Saint Marguerite d'Youville and the sisters of the Saint-Hyacinthe community have been faithfully preserved by the congregation's archivists. These documents comprised a powerful legacy which encouraged the Lewiston community to persevere. Nevertheless the practical demands of their ministry drove the Lewiston mission into debt.

The sisters did not turn to the Portland Diocese for debt relief. Instead they asked the French Canadian women of Saint Pierre parish, and the general Catholic laity of Lewiston, for financial and material assistance. The Grey Nuns also maintained a connection to Reverend Pierre Hevey following his departure from Lewiston to Manchester, New Hampshire in 1881.

Hevey was replaced by a community of three Dominican priests who arrived in Lewiston from Lille, France in 1881. The order assumed authority for Saint Pierre parish, cemetery and debt from the Portland Diocese.[4] Although there is no surviving data that details the changing of the parish name from Saint Pierre to Saints Pierre and Paul; chronologically this alteration occurred with the arrival of the Dominicans. The first Dominican pastor of Saints Pierre and Paul was the Reverend Alexander Louis Mothon, OP. His assistants were Fathers Constant Adam, OP and Ange Toutain, OP. Mothon was pastor of the parish for three administrations: 1881–1884, 1887–1897 and 1902–1906.[5]

Hevey's continued interest in the Grey Nuns' foundations led him to invest $12,000 in a venture capital arrangement with the sisters, on March 23, 1891, ten years after his departure from Lewiston.[6] The Grey Nuns seemingly preferred to enter into a contractual arrangement with Hevey, even on exploitative terms, rather than accept economic dependency upon the Portland See. This decision did somewhat handicap the power of the Portland bishop to control the sisters' activities through monetary channels, which seemed favorable, though less than fiscally advantageous, for the Grey Nuns. The efforts by independent women religious communities to avoid or minimize control of their missions by male clergy required strong leadership and skilled sister-accountants. Such actions usually resulted in difficult choices for the order. As one female religious scholar points out, "the question of authority of the community versus that of a local bishop was, perhaps, the single most important factor in the difficulties that arose as the sisters within each community moved from pioneer grouping to more structured institutions."[7]

As parochial educators at the Dominican Block, the Grey Nuns received minimal compensation. While this minor source of income allowed the Grey Nuns some degree of autonomy, it drained the sisters' resources for pursuing their primary vocation as a community of sister-nurses. The strength of their identity as sister-nurses and belief in their abilities to establish a hospital in Lewiston was ultimately incorporated into their first Hospital Annual Report for the year of 1893: "This institution, founded in 1888, is in charge of the Sisters of Charity, whose special calling is to care for the sick and needy. The Hospitals taken care of by this order in Montreal and Quebec are admitted, on all sides, to be second to none, on this continent."[8]

Not until the arrival of two more Catholic teaching-sister communities, the Sisters of Sion in 1892–1904, and Le Congregation de St. Dominique de Nancy in 1904, were the Grey Nuns relieved of their formal teaching responsibilities to French Canadian children outside of their orphanages. The sisters did continue, however, to be a presence in the life of Saint Pierre and Paul's parish community.

According to the order's journal's records, by the end of August 1888 the order had a balance of $15,802.17. Yet by the beginning of the following month, September, the balance was reduced to $383.96.[9] No accounting or explanation was recorded in the journal's ledger for this withdrawal. The absence of this money however corresponded to the Grey Nuns' initial

Figure 10: The Golder House between the 1902 Hospital General Sainte-Marie and the Asylum Wing.

down payment on the purchase of a house and thirty-six acre estate, known as the Sarah J. Golder Estate. Figure 10 shows the original Golder House between the Asylum wing on its left and the 1902 Hospital General Sainte-Marie on its right. The purchase was verified in the order's chronicle, in the amount of $22,000.[10]

The signer on the deeds for the Sisters of Charity was Sister Saint Charles, who simply signed the document as the "President of The Asylum of Our Lady of Lourdes."[11] By this signature, a French Canadian sister had become the first CEO of the first Lewiston hospital. Prior to her profession as a Grey Nun, the Asylum President's name was Helen Hogue. She was born in Sherbrooke, Quebec on September 27, 1843. Hogue entered the religious life at Saint-Hyacinthe in 1860 and professed on August 26, 1862. She lived thirty-nine years as a woman religious, dying at the age of fifty-eight on January 2, 1901.[12] The boldness of Sister Saint Charles and her Nuns was balanced by their recognition of the prejudices that surrounded them. The beginning of their hospital founding in Lewiston was recorded in the order's annals with the following commentary: "We felt instinctively the deep aversion of these old Puritans at the mere thought [that] the first institution for the care of the sick would be entrusted to ladies whose names and habits aroused suspicions."[13]

The Sarah J. Golder estate included a large Victorian house located on Sabbatus and Pine Streets on the outskirts of nineteenth-century Lewiston. In the sisters' own words, the Golder location was "in the suburbs of the city, commanding a magnificent view, overlooking the twin cities of Lewiston and Auburn. It is situated in the midst of a vast estate, where quiet reigns and wherein a clear and healthy atmosphere makes it an ideal spot for such an institution."[14] Once the real estate transaction was finalized, the sisters began an immediate renovation of the Golder house. The private home was remodeled as a hospital that included a long-term care facility. The girls' orphanage, part of the original house, was located at one end of the structure. The first printed annual report of the hospital set the "price of board" for the patients at "three dollars and fifty cents per week, in the common wards, and one or two dollars per day, in private rooms, according to accommodations."[15] The cost of private rooms increased annually until the new Hospital General Sainte-Marie finished construction in 1902. By the turn of the century the cost ranged between ten or twelve dollars per week. Cost varied according to the room's location in the hospital. These private rooms were comfortably furnished in the style of the period and the occupant was allowed to receive the benefits of personal care from private medical and domestic sources.[16] Providing private rooms to patients who possessed the financial means to pay for their hospitalization and treatment represented a secure source of income that, in turn, allowed the Grey Nuns to provide free care to the poorest patients. If a patient was on one of the wards, the hospitalization weekly charge included both board, medical and surgical attendance by the hospital staff.[17] The nursing care was provided freely and unconditionally.

The transformation of large Victorian houses into hospitals was a common practice in the nineteenth century. Patients were grouped together on single sex wards that were placed under the authority of a sister-nurse. Not until the twentieth century was the majority of hospital buildings origninally designed and built to be medical facilities. This was the scenario that occurred with the Grey Nuns' medical facilities in Lewiston. The Asylum of Our Lady of Lourdes was replaced with a building specifically designed and built as a hospital in 1902, the Hospital General Sainte-Marie.

Once the renovations were completed the remodeled Golder estate became a thirty-six bed hospital divided into two wards, one for female patients and the other for male. The sisters lived on the top floor and in the orphanage. Thirty of the beds were designated for short-term patients with six private rooms for either long-term paying patients, boarders or the wealthy. By November, the Golder house had become the Asylum of Our Lady of Lourdes and/or the Sister's Hospital to the populace of Lewiston. It was also known in Quebec as Lewiston's Saint-Hyacinthe Hospital.[18]

As the frost of a Maine November settled upon the Asylum of Our Lady of Lourdes, fifteen Grey Nuns, accompanied by forty girls identified as "orphans" who were in their care, quietly moved into the first hospital complex in Lewiston. The first Grey Nuns at the Asylum of Our Lady of Lourdes were: Eugenie Archambault, Emilie Bengle, Elizabeth Bouchard, Malvina Bourbonniere, Marie-Rose Bourgeois, Sophie Brault, Honorine Brodeur, Marie Casavant, Zéphyrine Duhamel, Zoé Langlois, Adeline Leblanc, Marie-Elizabeth Leduc, Georgiana Morin, Justine Perras, and Rosalie Surette. The first Superior was Sister Justine Perras. Sister Justine served in this role for the next three years. She was followed by four subsequent Superiors over the next nine years: Sisters Adeline Bernard (1891–1893); Adeline Leblanc (1893–1897); Cordelie Dorual (1897–1898); and Dorila Peltier (1898–1900). As will be seen, this rapid turnover during the first years of the Grey Nuns' hospital, did not affect the success of their efforts, including building a brand new hospital building.

The Protestant medical elite of Lewiston did not judge this facility as a hospital, but rather, as an "orphanage with hospital wards attached."[19] The first patient of record in the Grey Nuns' hospital was Nellie Hackett, who was admitted to Our Lady of Lourdes the following January in

1889.[20] Nellie Hackett was not, however, the first patient cared for by the Grey Nuns. As testified in their registry, the Grey Nuns had been administering and providing nursing services and care for the previous eight years. The official dedication of the Asylum by the Portland bishop did not occur until April 28, 1889.

The dedication of the Asylum of Our Lady of Lourdes was a day of firsts in the history of Maine. The first African American Catholic bishop was joined by the first female chief executive of a Maine hospital to dedicate the first hospital in Lewiston and the first Catholic hospital in Maine. The New England-educated Bishop James A. Healy was born in Georgia. His father had been a white Irish immigrant planter and his mother had been a slave. Healy was highly educated and did not practice an aggressive program of Americanization in his diocese. In fact throughout his episcopacy, Healy's written correspondences with the Grey Nuns were in their native French, not English.[21]

Unlike the ACMA board members, the Grey Nuns did not initially seek city and/or government aid for their hospital founding. What the sisters wanted and needed, however, was the acceptance of their institution by Lewiston's local medical community beyond the small staff of French Canadian physicians under the leadership of Dr. L.J. Martel. In addition to Martel, the first medical staff in the sisters' hospital consisted of the physicians Len Matte, Phidias Vanier and Sigebert Dumont.[22] Unfortunately the Yankee medical community would take years before they accepted the sisters' offer to provide medical care to the poor and ill in their hospital. This overt bigotry and sexism occurred even though nineteen years prior to the establishment of the sisters' hospital in Lewiston, the American Medical Association had "recognized nuns as the only organized group that realized the importance of nursing."[23]

With the support of the Catholic population of Lewiston, the Grey Nuns aggressively and consistently fought to provide health care in their hospital facility. With the founding of the Asylum of Our Lady of Lourdes, the Grey Nuns established a hospital staffed by nursing-sisters that not only welcomed Lewiston's Catholics, French Canadians and working poor, but was also open to the entire state. The sisters reaffirmed their commitment as sister-nurses and caregivers to the Lewiston community and the entire population of Maine in their annual mission statement: "This institution is non-sectarian. No distinction is made in regards to creed or nationality."[24]

Our Lady of Lourdes was a testament to the Grey Nuns' abilities as fundraisers, marketers and administrators. Furthermore it was the first fruit of their passion to work as a community of sister-nurses in Lewiston. The Grey Nuns declared that their "special training qualified them to perform the duties required, and to this calling they have devoted their lives."[25] Yet as the sisters wrote in their annales, the following decade was not one that brought acceptance of their hospital by the non-French Canadian medical community in Lewiston: "Non-Catholic physicians boycotted and prevented non-Catholic patients from entering the hospital. The most malicious innuendoes were circulated concerning the sisters. Rumors were spread that the medical organization was poor."[26]

The physicians of the ACMA who staffed Central Maine General Hospital freely admitted their bigotry. In the first annual report of Central Maine General Hospital the board reported that:

> "Our French Catholics saw their opportunity if they did not fully comprehend our need. The Sisters of Charity built an orphanage with hospital wards attached, and these were open to Catholic and Protestant patients alike, and the Androscoggin County Medical Association was invited to assume the medical and surgical care of them. This offer was a surprise. Was it best to accept it? Was this institution now and prospectively to answer our expectations? After careful consideration the offer was unanimously declined."

Figure 11: The First Site of Central Maine General Hospital.

Although the Central Maine General Hospital board admitted that their decision was "rude and ungracious" they felt it was justified upon the grounds that "only a hospital absolutely non-sectarian, to which State aid could be rendered, could expect to receive such support and patronage from our community."[27]

The position of the Central Maine General Hospital board directly ignored the sisters' mission statement, and was hypocritical, considering that in 1892 the eighth largest source of income in their own institution was "Sunday collections." The following year, Central Maine General Hospital was again the recipient of funds solicited through "Church Collections."[28] In 1896 the Central Maine General Hospital directors expressed their gratitude, for a $10,000 fund-raiser, to the "Women's Christian Temperance Union of Lewiston" whose contribution ranked as one of the hospital's "larger subscription[s]."[29] The women in the Christian Temperance Union were drawn predominantly from the Protestant elite of Lewiston.

The discrimination practiced by the ACMA resulted in hardship. Both the Grey Nuns and their institution suffered. But the Grey Nuns did not surrender. Rather they found an alternative to mitigate the bigotry. Canadian interns from Quebec were invited to train in their American hospital. The sisters also allowed their wealthier patients to have their own private physicians come to the hospital and provide medical care. Finally, through medical knowledge gained through long years of nursing and care giving, the sisters healed their patients directly themselves without employing a physician.

True to their vows and dedication to the virtue of humility, the Grey Nuns in their public accounts recorded these years of bigotry and suffering as only a time of "Hardship." In the 1902 commemorative annual hospital report celebrating the opening of Hospital General Sainte-Marie a historical overview was written of the Grey Nuns' ministry in Lewiston. In the article, the past years were reduced to a fable:

> "Here History comes in, and you know she is the sister deity to Justice, the blind woman. She relates sad things, speaks of a dreadful opposition that was aroused against the Sister's Hospital and so forth. Let it suffice to mention the fact without illustrating exactly what it was, and simply state that for months and years the Sisters had to experience what is really the, *bread and butter struggle for life*."[30]

Despite the use of sentimental language, the bigotry that the sisters suffered on account of the ACMA was not totally masked. The fact that the hardships were even mentioned by the sisters, in the words of a former Grey

Nun superior, "testifies that the severity of the discrimination that these women suffered was so severe that it could not be silenced by their prayers."[31] Through this article the Grey Nuns, a foreign community of women religious, voiced in their own subtle way their recognition of the injustice they had endured in America. This action bespoke a determination to own their personal history and achievements in Lewiston. The Grey Nuns were challenging the myopic worldview of acceptable nineteenth-century female behavior, as well as the prevailing ethnic stereotypes. The societal norms of Lewiston's Yankee culture had failed to quash the Grey Nuns' influence and their institutions.

Understanding their hardships in the light of divine suffering on their faith journey, the sisters persevered against the ACMA and other bigotry. Their hospital not only survived but grew under its female leadership and administration. During the first years, those who sought the Grey Nuns' care were never turned away, even if it "necessitated the placing of extra beds" in the wards.[32] The sisters' open admission policy welcomed all who suffered regardless of the nature of the illness. This was dramatically demonstrated when typhoid fever struck the rural Maine communities of Rumford Falls, Jay and Livermore Falls in 1896. Of the twenty-five fever victims that were admitted to the sisters' hospital, twenty-four had "satisfactory results."[33] Contrary to the Grey Nuns' open admission policy, the directors of Central Maine General Hospital practiced a selective admission policy:

> "[I]f it is anything of a contagious or incurable nature the application is at once denied, as this hospital is not intended for cases of that kind. Only acute and curable cases are taken . . . and more good can be done by the admission of such patients as are curable than by filling up the wards and rooms with a class whose cases are hopeless."[34]

THE SISTERS OF CHARITY, INCORPORATED

In 1892, the sisters recognized that the security and long-term growth of their institution required adaptation to the legalism of the United States. Just as the ACMA leadership had incorporated themselves and their hospital into Central Maine General Hospital in 1891, the Grey Nuns incorporated themselves and their four-year-old institution into the Hospital of the Society of the Sisters of Charity of Lewiston, Maine on July 2, 1892.[35] This action by the Grey Nuns was indicative of their growing understanding of American culture as well as their success at controlling their own process of self-Americanization.[36] The incorporation of the Grey Nuns of Saint-Hyacinthe into the Sisters of Charity of Lewiston did not alter their internal structure or their religious self-understanding of the congregation as an "educational, benevolent and charitable organization." Furthermore, the community continued canonically as The Sisters of Charity of Saint-Hyacinthe, Grey Nuns, despite their legal incorporation as the Sisters of Charity of Lewiston.

Almost a year prior to the July 2, 1892 incorporation of the Asylum of Our Lady of Lourdes, the Grey Nuns and Father Hevey had drawn up a financial contract. The document, *The Engagement of the Asylum of Our Lady of Lourdes with Monsignor Hevey and the Sisters for the sum of $12,000, March 23, 1891* regards the terms and fiduciary responsibility agreed upon by the Grey Nuns for the sum of $12,000 which Hevey "gave" to the order for their hospital. This financial contract provides illumination of the relationship between the sisters, clergy and of the time. According to the document, the Grey Nuns accepted a sum of $12,000 with the following conditions:

> "First, The money had to stay with the order forever. No one, including Hevey, had the right to ask for the return of the donation. Second, the amount of $12,000 shall produce an interest payment of 6 percent or $720, which will be payable to Hevey, semi-annually during his lifetime.[37] Upon Hevey's death his interest payment would be divided and paid semi-annually to his surviving brothers, sister and sisters-in-law, [at the time, this included six people]. Finally the community could, at its sole discretion, retain the $720 payment and not pay Hevey or his attorney. If this option was chosen and the Grey Nuns did not give Hevey the interest payment of $720, then the order would have to pay 5 percent of the $720 annually as rent to Hevey's niece."[38]

One of the most striking elements in this document is the use of the term donation, which is defined as "the action or contract by which a person transfers the ownership of a thing from them self to another as a free gift."[39] In actuality what was donated to the Grey Nuns was the use of $12,000 for which they had to pay at least a nominal sum to either Hevey or his niece. Supporting the Grey Nuns was an investment of venture capital for Hevey and his family and not an act of philanthropy. Yet if the Grey Nuns were to proceed with their benevolent ambitions to establish a hospital for the suffering poor while retaining their autonomy, their options were financially and legally limited in nineteenth-century America. Both their gender and nationality were permanently against them and their foundation. Furthermore the cultural prejudice which the sisters endured as Catholic women religious limited their access to secular sources of capital. This monetary arrangement was one of their few choices. Unfortunately, the Grey Nuns' situation was not uncommon in the American Church, as the exploitation of women religious by male clergy was prevalent during the nineteenth century. At this time, members of the male clergy often required sisters to be rectory housekeepers in addition to their teaching and nursing responsibilities. Also not rare was the habit among the male clergy to acquire control of, if not outright title to, the money and property of female religious.

Despite the financial assistance from Hevey and the minimal compensation for working at Saint Pierre parish, the Grey Nuns continued to be burdened with economic hardship. To preserve their autonomy, the order did not physically or geographically attach its convent to a parish, or place the community under direct diocesan authority. By choosing to retain their ties to the motherhouse in Saint-Hyacinthe and not structurally integrating into the Portland See, the Grey Nuns continually faced poverty. Their critical need for money to sustain their community and foundations would lead the Directress of the Girls' Orphanage to appeal, as late as 1908: "It is in favor of these children [girls who had no relatives] that the Sisters of Charity are obligated to make special calls upon the charity of their good friends, who not only give out of their pockets, but will go all over Lewiston in search of the public money."[40]

In addition to "making special calls" or begging, the sisters supported themselves and their institutions in a number of ways. As recorded in the order's journal and other documents, the sisters taught, nursed, sewed, cooked, cleaned, sheltered and cared for children. The need of the Grey Nuns to acquire funding for their ministry fostered their independence, creativity, aggressiveness, and managerial and organizational skills. If the Grey Nuns were to survive in Lewiston, the sisters had to develop a public relations campaign that skillfully marketed their community's talents as nurses, educators, artisans and welfare providers, while not drawing anti-Catholic animosity towards them. In light of the fact that the Grey Nuns in 1878 did not speak the English language, adhered to the tenets of the foreign Catholic faith, and belonged to a gender that was treated subserviently in American society and within Catholicism, their achievements are all the more astounding.

What the Grey Nuns did have on their side was the moral credibility of their habit. As veiled women, their behavior was not interpreted as violating the social norms of appropriate feminine activities. By physically masking themselves, they gained a cultural form of power that was socially tolerated. In marketing terminology, the Grey Nuns' habit was a trademark that guaranteed to the public that these women lived in a real and deep communion with God. They were not interpreted as challengers to the authority of Victorian norms that fostered misogynistic feelings towards woman. Their habits thus granted them permission to live autonomously and not in sexist oppression. Their actions were often judged as a manifestation of their spiritual authority as "Brides of Christ." This in turn gave the sisters a public power that they did not hesitate to use for the benefit of their ambitions.

The Grey Nuns recognized and used this power. Between 1888 and 1894, the medical and surgical care at the Asylum of Our Lady of Lourdes expanded dramatically. In these six years the Asylum successfully treated 630 patients and suffered only 57 deaths. The following chapter will examine the specific illnesses of the Grey Nuns' patients. The success of the Grey Nun's health care ministry, represented by its 92 percent survival rate, was finally recognized by Lewiston's medical community. The Grey Nuns' annals record that: "Opposition to the hospital gradually ceased and acceptance of American patients and American doctors started. These doctors were welcome and well received."[41] This acceptance of the Asylum by the medical community was recorded in the 1894 annual report, in which the sisters' listed eight consulting physicians and surgeons, four attending surgeons, two adjunct surgeons and four attending physicians. The hospital staff totaled eighteen physicians of whom eight had English or Irish surnames.[42]

In 1893 a committee of physicians from Lewiston traveled to Augusta and sought state support for the sisters' hospital. After the initial appeal was unsuccessful, the Lewiston committee regrouped to include supporters that were drawn from a variety of professional and geographical areas. This second attempt succeeded. The State of Maine agreed to award $1,250 in a form of a yearly grant to the Asylum of Our Lady of Lourdes.[43] Although this grant represented only 5 percent of the State funding that Central Maine General Hospital was receiving by 1893, it signified the political, social and professional recognition of the Grey Nuns' hospital by the Maine polity.[44]

While the Grey Nuns were acquiring political and business acumen as American hospital founders, administrators and nurses they dealt with an outside world defined by gender, clerical, and professional authority. This "male only" boundary required that the sisters become negotiators if their hospital was to remain autonomous. They had to learn to balance the professional, religious and sexist attitudes held towards sister-nurses and caregivers, while maintaining their authority as directors of a Catholic female medical institution. They skillfully used their image as humble veiled holy women to merge seamlessly into their hospital wards, and thus secured their right to be present from both patient and physician. Their behavior was noted by the editor of the hospital's 1902 Annual Report: "Sisters of Charity [Grey Nuns] never have their pictures made individually, and even if you happen to find one of them in a group, she will either be way back in the rear and in the shade, or will turn her face from you."[45]

While Sister Saint Charles had used her own religious name when signing the 1888 registry deed, her successors simply used "Superior" when signing the hospital's annual reports. Yet the male physicians who practiced at the sisters' hospital were prominently listed in the first pages of every annual report. When the hospital surgeon and chief of staff Alonzo Garcelon died, he received a full page memorial in the 1906 Hospital Annual Report, an honor never bestowed upon any Grey Nun.[46] Furthermore the Grey Nuns were not economically compensated for their work as sister-nurses, administrators, pharmacists, and technicians in the hospital. They made no demands upon either medical or church authorities for financial compensation. Their extreme selflessness was judged by the

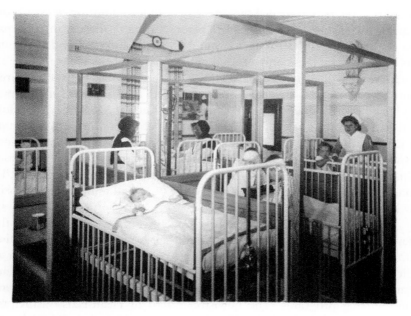

Figure 12: Sister-Nurses Working in the Pediatrics Ward in the 1920s, Virtually Unchanged since 1902.

Maine political elite as unique. When State Representative S.J. Kelley first visited the Asylum of Our Lady of Lourdes, he commented: "The thing which struck me most forcibly about the whole affair is the fact that no one around the institution draws a salary—not a single individual."[47]

Even though the sisters lacked economic compensation for their endeavors, the form of anonymity which the Grey Nuns practiced gave them valuable negotiating tools. The "good sister" who worked in the silence of her hospital wards, living a devoted life in a consecrated religious community, was not perceived as a threat by either secular or religious authority. This in turn gave the sisters the ability to proceed with their nursing and care ambitions with minimal outside interference.

While the Grey Nuns' hospital was initially ignored by Lewiston's Yankee medical community, the people of Lewiston aggressively sought out the sisters' care. The number of patients admitted to the hospital per year grew from 160 in 1893 to 1,235 in 1908.[48] By the middle of the last decade of the nineteenth century, the Asylum of Our Lady of Lourdes was straining to meet the public's demand for hospital services. Infectious disease, industrial accidents, birth complications, childhood illness, the effects of poor nutrition, exhaustion, and overwork were not only the lower-class reality, but also plagued the emerging middle class. In the Grey Nuns' annual reports, they recorded the diversity of illness, duration of stay, costs of medical and surgical services, birth place, current residence, and occupation of their patients. Between 1893 and 1898 the sisters provided care to 1,546 patients. Of these only 46 died in the sisters' care.[49] This represents a 3 percent mortality rate. In consideration of the fact that the staff of Grey Nuns never exceeded nineteen sisters at a time, a 97 percent survival rate was a significant achievement. In comparison Central Maine General Hospital had a survival rate of 95.7 percent out of a total of 1,938 patients during the same period.[50] The most common medical conditions of those hospitalized at Hospital General Sainte-Marie were: typhoid fever, bronchitis, acute diarrhea, neurasthenia, and "uterus curetted and dilated."[51] None of these illnesses were exclusive to the poor and immigrant classes of Lewiston.

Furthermore the demand in Lewiston for nursing performed by the Grey Nun sister-nurses was not limited to their hospital wards. Remaining faithful to their original mission, the sisters continued to "visit the poor in their homes." An interesting parallel exists between the Grey Nuns' nineteenth-century home nursing visits and contemporary hospice care and home nursing programs. The Lewiston Board of Health also asked the Grey Nuns to fulfill the duties of public nurses, which they did whenever asked.

The population of Lewiston suffered two significant smallpox epidemics, the first in 1900 and the second in 1905. The most serious cases of smallpox were removed to the city-maintained pest house, which was at that time a small wooden building on the River Road close to the Catholic Cemetery of Mount Hope that was attached to Saint Joseph Parish. The Lewiston Board of Health asked for, and the Grey Nuns agreed to supply, 162 days of nursing at the city pest house in 1900 and 1903 and another 65 days in 1905, an obligation they fulfilled.[52] The Board of Health did not make a similar request for nursing services from Central Maine General Hospital. The Grey Nuns fulfilled this nursing obligation to the patients of the pest house despite the demand it required upon their limited time. This situation eventually required them "to refuse other calls from outside [the hospital] for the same line of work, except in a few instances."[53]

By 1899 cost of hospitalization at Hospital General Sainte-Marie was five dollars per week for the general wards.[54] Children were admitted to adult wards since separate pediatric care was still in its infancy. In addition to the accounts of paying patients, the hospital also received financial support from not only the Catholic female lay Association of the Ladies of Charity but also the Lady Patronesses Hospital Society, which was open to the Catholic laity and secular public beginning in 1898.[55] In 1899 the Patrons' Society was established to recognize and strengthen the contribution from the lay and secular male population of Lewiston. The combined fundraising of these societies amounted to $611.25 in 1899. The appropriation from the State Legislature had continued since 1893 and was expanded to $3,000 in 1899. The financial support from local charities and the state allowed the sisters to continue to "treat gratis" those patients who could not afford the expense of hospitalization.

In 1893 the sisters recorded 128 admissions to their hospital with an additional 40 children to their orphanage. By 1899 the hospital admissions had increased to 352 or more than doubling in six years. Of the 352 patients admitted to the hospital between December 1898 to December 1899, 102, or 29 percent of the patients were "treated gratis." Another 84 patients, or 24 percent of those admitted were "part pay." So 53 percent of all those admitted to the Asylum of Our Lady of Lourdes over this period were either treated without charge by the sisters or only made partial payment towards the cost of their hospitalization.[56] The next chapter contains a comparison of patient financing for both Lewiston hospitals.

The nationality of the patients was not consistently recorded in the annual reports from 1893–1908. The reports do provide, however, sufficient information to construct a general portrait of a few immigrants and their families. One such woman was Jeanne Carpentier along with her husband and children from Bath, Maine. Jeanne and her family's involvement with the Asylum of Our Lady of Lourdes is traced out in the following chapter.

The Grey Nuns' commitment as health care providers to Lewiston would include by 1899 the opening of a drop-in clinic for the treatment of eye, ear, nose and throat ailments. As previously discussed, the harsh environmental conditions of mill work and tenement life damaged many laborers' visual and respiratory systems. The clinic was directed by an ophthalmic specialist whom the hospital had engaged. The sisters called this clinic their "outdoor department," a predecessor of the modern "innovation" of outpatient clinics. By the end of 1899 the clinic had treated 289 patients.[57] In spite of the success of their "outdoor department," the hospital wards were still inadequate. The public demand for medical care had outgrown the sisters' facilities. According to the 1899 Annual Report, for the first time in the history of the Asylum, "a large number of applicants who sought admission to the Hospital had to be refused owing to lack of accommodations."[58] The sisters had to either expand their current hospital or construct a new facility. They chose the latter. In 1898 the sisters decided to construct a new hospital.[59] This would be a modern medical facility that could meet the public's increasing demand for professionalized medical care, while fulfilling the sisters' vision of an institution that cared for the suffering poor.

By the end of 1899, the Grey Nuns had prepared an aggressive plan to build a new hospital separate from the Asylum of our Lady of Lourdes but still located on the Sarah Golder estate. Within a year, architectural plans had been drawn and fundraising began. The Lewiston architect William R. Miller was selected by the sisters and the Dominican architect Reverend Paul Charland, OP was also consulted. The sisters and architects agreed upon a three-story brick building distinguished by two octagonal towers that dominated the corners of the front and west side elevations. One tower was designated for the surgery and the other tower became the hospital chapel. The wards were located between the two towers and opened onto the chapel. The windows and entrances are symmetrical in placement.

Once the design was completed for the new hospital, the Grey Nuns again exercised their quiet diplomacy by inviting the Bishop Healy to review the hospital plans and the community's finances. The sisters did not require the bishop's approval for their ambitions as they remained independent and in fact had already begun to bring this medical foundation into reality with or without it. This invitation, however, was an astute tactical move since if successful it would obtain the support of the Bishop, the diocesan clergy and the wealth members of the Maine Catholic laity. Bishop Healy found "the finances of the Sisters [were] in sufficiently good order to warrant the erection of a new and modern hospital."[60] Money for the hospital construction came from the sisters' savings that had been collected through harsh years of begging, laboring over attractive devotional booklets for the laity, child care services provided at their orphanage, French language lessons given in the privacy of their own convent to wealthier girls, teaching in the Dominican Block, and working for the Dominican fathers. There were also public fundraising events that involved the entire Lewiston community. Construction of this ambitious project was launched only twelve years from the opening of the Asylum of Our Lady of Lourdes.

Chapter Seven
Portrait of a Patient

The success of the Asylum of Our Lady of Lourdes required an honest approach by the Grey Nuns to the realities of poverty, immigration and industrialization as it existed in the growing industrial urban center that was nineteenth-century Lewiston. As illustrated by patient occupations listed in the record books of the Asylum of Our Lady of Lourdes, the Grey Nuns' patients were predominantly from the immigrant working class. For example, in the 1896 Annual Report, the Grey Nuns recorded the occupations of their patients. The majority of the 300 patients in 1896 were listed as: "Factory girls, House maids, Weavers, Laborers, Servants and Miners."[1]

Though the income that the wage-labor class earned in the Lewiston mills was more than the income from subsistence farming and most other menial jobs, it came at a high cost to the worker. The unhealthful conditions that existed in the textile mills from polluted air and deafening noise, dangerous machinery, and long, exhausting shifts spent in poorly lighted, damp and/or overly heated rooms had negative consequences for workers' short and long-term health. This will be examined in much more detail in the next chapter. The exhausting Monday through Saturday work week also limited mill workers' access to timely medical care and their ability to recuperate from injury.

Furthermore, economic security was elusive at best for the wage laborer and the newly arrived immigrants. Not only was absenteeism not tolerated, but workers were subject to fines and other pay reductions without recourse. If a child care crisis arose, economic security could be unattainable. Without a source of income or welfare assistance, poverty and dependency could quickly become a reality for a wage laborer and/or immigrant and their dependent family. This in turn had psychological and physical consequences for the family, especially since the only public alternatives

Figure 13: Bates Mill Spinning Room Workers.

were Lewiston's city farm or alms house. The Grey Nuns had reached out to Petit Canada's families immediately upon their arrival, although with limited means for extended child care. Once the Grey Nuns founded the Asylum of Our Lady of Lourdes and the Healy Asylum, immigrant families had additional support in their times of need. If a family's dependent children could be placed with the Grey Nuns at either the girls' orphanage of Asylum of Our Lady of Lourdes or at the Healy Asylum; the parent and/or parents (as was often the case) were free to seek economic stability or regain their health. If a family continued to be in crisis, was a single parent family, or required both parents to earn a living, the sisters often "took" the children on "their own responsibility." In a letter dated March 2, 1900, between Reverend Edward Hurley of Saint Dominic's Church, Portland and Bishop Healy, the Grey Nuns are credited with maintaining children from two families at their own cost; one of whom was "protestant."[2]

The Grey Nuns' understanding of care was extended to the entire families of the suffering poor and included not only illnesses but the effects of poverty. The admissions and length of stay of one particular family, the Carpentiers, provide a case study of the Grey Nuns' inclusive health care ministry. The Carpentiers were French immigrants by way of Canada, as opposed to French Canadian as were most immigrant families at this time in Lewiston and the Grey Nuns themselves. Their original Maine residence was in the town of Bath, approximately 50 miles east of Lewiston. Records indicate that their education level and occupation were probably higher than the average patient at the Asylum of Our Lady of Lourdes. Yet in spite of these differences, their story resonates with some of the same experiences shared by the poorest, most humbly educated Quebecois farmer who arrived in Lewiston via the Grand Trunk Railway. In fact, these differences speak volumes about the region-wide, if not statewide, impact of the works of the Grey Nuns, as the Carpentiers clearly sought out the immigrant sisters from Saint-Hyacinthe to help them in their difficulties.

The reason for the initial admission of the Carpentier family to the Asylum of Our Lady of Lourdes was not recorded by the Grey Nuns in their register. Instead, only the dates of admission, the family's baptismal information, and their dates of discharge were recorded by the sisters. This lack of detailed information regarding a patient's physical condition, while emphasizing the patient's sacramental life, was not an uncommon practice in late nineteenth-century Catholic hospitals. As previously discussed, the Grey Nuns and other women religious were equally concerned with their patients' spiritual condition as they were with their physical condition. (records were maintained by the Grey Nuns of the type and number of generalized medical conditions presented at their hospital.)[3] Nursing-sisters, however, did not feel the need to tie a patient's admissions record to the specific medical treatment required or received. In fact, this minimalist approach to record keeping was the norm at both the Hospital General Sainte-Marie and the Central Maine General Hospital during this period.[4]

At the time of their initial admission, the Carpentier family consisted of a father, mother, son and daughter. All four family members were admitted by the sisters on March 14, 1891.[5] The parents, George Carpentier and Jeanne Montez Carpentier, must have been French immigrants, who most likely grew up together in or near the same town in France. The Grey Nuns' records indicate that both parents were baptized in the same city, Dunkerque (Dunkirk), located on the extreme northern coast of France, in the Pas de Calais. After their marriage, the Carpentiers had a son, George Emmanuel, while apparently still living in France. The family moved to Brittany, the westernmost province of France, at some point. They stayed in Brittany long enough for George Emmanuel to receive the sacrament of baptism in the city of Rennes. Rennes is about 300 miles southwest of Dunkerque. After this event, the family then emigrated to Canada, settling in Montreal. Their first daughter, Marie Theresa, was most likely born in Canada, since the records indicate that she was baptized in Montreal. These records do not indicate when the Carpentiers immigrated to the United States, but they most likely took passage on the Grand Trunk Railway to Portland. In Portland the Carpentiers could have caught a local train to Bath, where they were living before their admission.

The entire family was discharged on the same date, March 16, 1891. It is extremely unlikely that the medical condition(s) which required their initial hospitalization was identically expressed by each family member. Nor is it probable that each family member responded to treatment with the exact same results, so they were all healthy at the time of discharge. What is very clear, however, is that the entire family received at least some care under the sisters' authority during these two days, whether medical or simply room and board. The entire family stayed at the Asylum of Our Lady of Lourdes as patients until the health of the ill members had improved sufficiently to be discharged from the hospital. It is possible, if not even likely, that perhaps the adult Carpentiers were both ill, with no child care for their two healthy children. One detail supporting this supposition can be found in the Grey Nuns' admission records. These minimalist records note that both adult Carpentiers were admitted sequentially, before their children. Then the family's admission record is interrupted by the record of the admission of another patient, the unnamed daughter of one Francois Bernier. Following this interruption, the records note the admission of both George Emmanuel and Maria Theresa sequentially.[6] If both

George and Jeanne Carpentier were ill enough to require hospitalization at the same time, their status in Bath, as newly arrived European immigrants, may have meant that they had yet to find a welfare network that could have provided adequate child care options for their two children. If this was the case, the Grey Nuns then provided room and board for both of the children until the parents had recovered sufficiently to be discharged. During this period in the development of their hospital, the sisters certainly understood the value and humanity in keeping families together, and commonly took such measures when necessary. Whatever the reason for the admission of George, Jeanne and their two children (and perhaps the reason was a happy one, as discussed below), what mattered to the Grey Nuns was not the particularities behind the Carpentiers' need for hospital care, but rather the rather simple fact that they *were* in need. The Grey Nuns did not discriminate between those who showed up on the doorstep. However, the fact that the Carpentiers and their children belonged to the French Catholic immigrant diaspora for which the sisters had been called to minister, must have resonated strongly with the French Canadian women immigrants who staffed and ran the Asylum of Our Lady of Lourdes.[7]

The Carpentier family apparently returned to Bath and resumed their lives. This life now included a second daughter, named Magdeleine. The Grey Nuns' records show that Magdeleine received the sacrament of baptism in Bath, most likely at the local Catholic church of Saint Mary's. Perhaps the birth of little Magdeleine was the reason for her parents' admission to the Asylum of Our Lady of Lourdes earlier in the year. If so, such holistic care for a pregnant woman and her family would be in keeping with the spirit of the Grey Nuns, which can still be seen today in the facilities and staff of the Dorothy LePage Womens' Pavilion at the contemporary Saint Mary's Regional Medical Center.

In any event, the entire Carpentier family, including little Magdeleine, was admitted again to the Asylum of Our Lady of Lourdes, only nine months after their prior stay. The five Carpentiers were all admitted by the sisters on December 12, 1891. Three weeks later, after the family spent Christmas in the hospital, George Carpentier was discharged by himself on January 2, 1892. Wife and mother Jeanne, brother George Emmanuel, sister Marie Theresa, and baby Magdeleine all remained behind. Jeanne and her three children remained in the sisters' care for almost another two months. All four were discharged together to a no doubt happy and relieved George, on February 27, 1892.[8] Once again, the Grey Nuns' records cannot be relied upon to answer the question of which member or members of the Carpentier family were ill. The hospital records cannot tell us even what the nature of their medical condition(s) might have been. Was one of the Carpentier children ill, or were perhaps all of the children suffering from a common complaint? Was mother Jeanne seriously ill enough to require a nearly three month hospital stay? Had she recently given birth to little Magdeleine and suffered severe complications or depression? Events lying in the future for this French immigrant family would shed only partial light on these questions.

For the immigrant Catholic, the other repository of personal and familial information was their parish church. Unfortunately for the story of the Carpentiers, the family's parish of Saint Mary's in Bath was severely damaged in a fire around 1900. As a result, there are no surviving sacramental records on the parishioners of Saint Mary's Church for the years between 1860 and 1900.[9] Ultimately, the answer to the question of why the Grey Nuns admitted the entire Carpentier family into their hospital twice in nine months will never be known. However, since during the second hospitalization, father George was discharged singly, it seems that he was not the reason for the entire family's admission. It also seems probable that if it were only one, or perhaps two of the children that required medical care, mother Jeanne may have been discharged with her healthy children, in order to care for them at home and keep as much of the family together as possible. Thus it would be reasonable to speculate that, as seen in the Asylum of Our Lady of Lourdes many times since, the sisters were providing child care for three healthy children while their father worked six days per week and their sick mother received medical treatment.

George Carpentier's occupation was listed in the admission records of the Asylum of Our Lady of Lourdes.[10] George was listed as a Civil Engineer.[11] Although engineering is a skilled position, George Carpentier was a Catholic Francophone immigrant in a Yankee world. It is still true even today that many non-English speaking immigrant professionals are unable to find employment in their chosen profession due to a language barrier or local prejudice. There are no assurances or any proof that George was able to find employment as a civil engineer. In fact, it is possible that his family's stays at the Asylum of Our Lady of Lourdes were at least in part due to financial considerations as much as their cultural comfort with a Catholic Francophone institution. In any event, George Carpentier would not have had any work-related health care benefits, such as sick leave or family disability. Such medical and welfare benefits in America were the creation of the second half of the twentieth century. In addition, the Carpentiers were originally from France, so it is unlikely that in Bath, Maine there would have been an established familiar network to provide care for the children or aid to the mother, even if there were Canadian Francophones nearby. The simple, but poignant fact is that on January 2, 1892, George Carpentier was

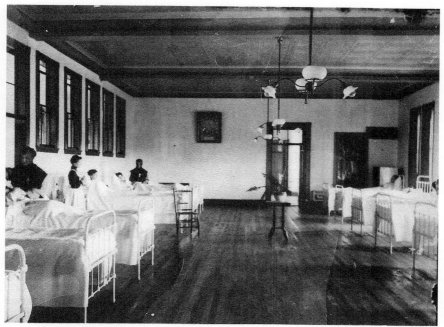

Figure 14: Womens' Ward, Sainte-Marie, 1902.

discharged even if he continued to have some chronic illness or disability, or even if he wished to stay with Jeanne and their children. George had little alternative but to return to work if his hospitalized family was to survive. He most likely returned to home and work in Bath, separated by at least a half day's journey from his family in Lewiston.

The records indicate that at least for some time in 1892, the Carpentier family was reunited. One can only imagine how Jeanne Carpentier felt to return to her home and family in her adopted country. While summers in Maine are normally beautiful, one hopes that the summer of 1892 was particularly beautiful, especially for the Carpentier family.

Unfortunately, the Carpentier family had to call again on the Grey Nuns for assistance. Only nine months after the Carpentier family's last discharge from the Asylum of Our Lady of Lourdes, the family was readmitted on November 28, 1892. This time however, only Jeanne Carpentier, son George and both daughters, Marie Theresa and Magdeleine, were admitted. The admission records again offer no details about the medical condition(s) driving their need for hospitalization. However, with a similar pattern as their last stay, in the hospitalization of only the mother and children, it seems likely that Jeanne Carpentier had some form of relapse. The fact that her last two hospitalizations occurred at roughly the same time of year leads one to believe that she may have had a chronic condition that worsened in the late fall. With George working long hours 50 miles away it made sense to keep the children at the Asylum. The children George, Marie Theresa and Magdeleine were all discharged on New Year's Day, 1893. But it must have been a cheerless holiday in the hospital, as their mother Jeanne had died on Christmas Eve, 1892.[12] Little Magdeleine must have been less than two years old.

What can be reasonably surmised from the information contained in the Carpentier family admission records was that the Grey Nuns practiced not just a flexible, but an open, admission policy in their hospital. The Grey Nuns' admission policy and, in fact their entire practice of their professions as health care providers and sister-nurses, drew from a healing tradition that gave support and security, individually and collectively to both patient and caregiver. This in turn, led to a more fluid understanding of the complexities of illness, poverty and marginalization. The objective of the Grey Nuns was to mitigate suffering and aid families in crisis, regardless of the particularities of the illness. The aid provided to the tragic Carpentier family allowed an apparently chronically ill woman to rest easier knowing that her children were nearby and in the care of women religious. It allowed a worrying father and husband to try to provide for his family, comforted by the fact that while he could not always be with them, his family was together and receiving the best of care. It allowed the children to spend time with their mother before her death, while also ensuring that their physical needs were being satisfied.[13]

The interior prayer life of a Grey Nun, her medical training in urban hospitals and her close relationship with the poor, all gave a Grey Nun a uniquely intimate understanding that the suffering poor had few options but death when stricken with serious illness. Their vocation to a life as women religious meant that they were responsible for bringing charity and healing to the suffering poor. A direct consequence of the Grey Nuns' inclusive and comprehensive approach to poverty and illness was that the Asylum of Our Lady of Lourdes evolved into a multi-care medical complex in the twentieth century. The institution built by immigrant women hidden in habits presented a health care challenge to the Protestant elite who controlled the Central Maine General Hospital and Lewiston's benevolent community. Their challenge resulted in lifting the quality of all health care for all people in Lewiston.

Chapter Eight

The Nuns and the Yankees

By constructing an analytical paradigm between Hospital General Sainte-Marie and Central Maine General Hospital, a clarification is achieved that illuminates the medical culture of care that existed in each institution between the years 1892–1908. The patient data reviewed for each hospital includes: ethnicity, gender, occupation, medical conditions presented, causes of death, survival rates, and financing (extent of charitable care). This data can be used to construct a better understanding of the actual hospital work performed by the Grey Nuns; and how their unique approach to benevolence was expressed by their nursing care in comparison to a secular, male-dominated Yankee establishment just a few miles away.

As detailed thus far, a new social welfare system was emerging in Lewiston that was being shaped by the practices of care and the religious identity of the Grey Nuns, while simultaneously being influenced by the professional and technological developments in American medicine. This created a dialectical interaction that involved issues of power, gender, religion, wealth and autonomy.

For a period of nine years, 1900–1908, the Grey Nuns recorded the nationality of their patients at Hospital General Sainte-Marie. From this information, an understanding of the ethnicity of their patients may be developed and compared to the ethnic make-up of Lewiston and Androscoggin County, as found in the 1910 Federal Census data for these jurisdictions discussed earlier. It is important to remember that these numbers do not reflect second or third generation ethnicity.[1]

The concentration of immigrants in Lewiston pales beside the immigrant population making up the bulk of Sainte-Marie's patients during the years 1900 to 1908 as shown in Figure 15. Canadian-born patients made up nearly 50 percent of the total patient population in Sainte-Marie, compared to 28 percent of the overall Lewiston population and only 18 percent

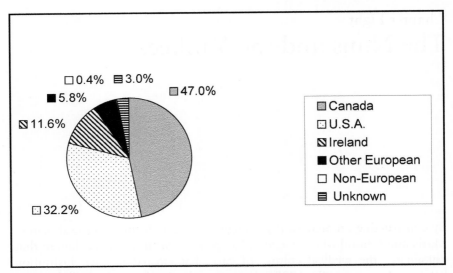

Figure 15: Patient Nativity, Sainte-Marie, 1900–1908.

of the Androscoggin County population. Unfortunately the nationality of the patients was not consistently recorded in the annual reports for Sainte-Marie from 1893–1900. Collectively, the reports do provide sufficient information to construct a general portrait of the nationalities of the Sainte-Marie patients for the years between 1900 and 1908, at both the end of this study period and the end of the boom period of French Canadian immigration. While 47 percent of patients were Canadian in origin, the other nationalities of the patients were Russian, Scottish, Italian, Irish, German, French, English, Jewish, and American.[2] The sisters gave "all patients . . . the same treatment and attention without regard to creed or nationality." In the order's own words, "the sisters . . . have devoted their lives to such work and their tenderness and skill in their vocation to facilitate the recovering of patients."[3]

In addition to the Canadian-born patients, the other established immigrant groups at this time were the Irish who comprised 12 percent of the hospital's patients, and other Europeans (primarily from the United Kingdom, Italy and Eastern Europe), who made up 6 percent of the patient population. This meant that immigrants made up almost two-thirds of all of Hospital General Sainte-Marie's patients, at a very late date for French Canadian immigration. As a comparison, the Twin Cities had only 29 percent immigrants in its population according to the 1910 census, while Androscoggin County had only 24 percent in its population. It is clear that immigrants overwhelmingly chose to be treated by the Grey Nuns.

Unfortunately Central Maine General Hospital did not report patient nationalities in its annual reports. Central Maine General did report the residences of its patients, but this categorization is not reliable enough to determine ethnicities, since it would under-report foreign-born patients who were residing in Maine. However, given the huge percent disparity between the immigrant population patronizing Sainte-Marie and the geographical jurisdictions in which they most likely lived, Central Maine General would have been hard-pressed to even reach similar percentages as Androscoggin County and the Twin Cities for its patient population. The simple fact is that the immigrant percentage at Sainte-Marie was about twice that of the general population, which indicates that these groups turned to the Grey Nuns for care, while Central Maine General Hospital undoubtedly served a predominantly Yankee clientele.

While the Hospital General Sainte-Marie was built, staffed and run by women, from its earliest days it has had a balanced gender mix for its patients. A review of the annual reports for Sainte-Marie from 1888 to 1910 indicates that in most years the gender ratio was fairly balanced. Results were typically close to 50:50, although in some early years this could be thrown off due to the small number of patients of either gender. Most years did have slightly more male patients than female, by about 55:45 or less. More interestingly, female patient mortality at Saint-Marie was typically higher than male patient mortality for virtually every year surveyed. This is not too surprising when the data on common causes of death is examined, since the number one cause of death was due to complications from obstetrical and gynecological conditions. This will be discussed at more length elsewhere in this chapter. Gender mortality rates did appear to be converging in the last years reviewed. The bottom line is that a patient walking out of Sainte-Marie was more likely to be male, while a deceased patient was more likely to be female.[4] Gender data was not reviewed for Central Maine General.

It is also possible to form a generalized picture of in-patient occupation, according to the patient's occupation, for a four-year consecutive period at each hospital.[5] Both hospitals at times recorded patient occupations. However, as they did not do so for all years between 1893 to 1908; it must be acknowledged that this data is sketchy and represents a different four year period for each institution.[6] Using a four-year average was an attempt at approaching the typical percentages of actual patient occupations seen at each hospital.

As we have seen, the Hospital General Sainte-Marie was founded, run and generally patronized by immigrants, which drew a patient population primarily made up of unskilled laborers, and secondarily made up of skilled

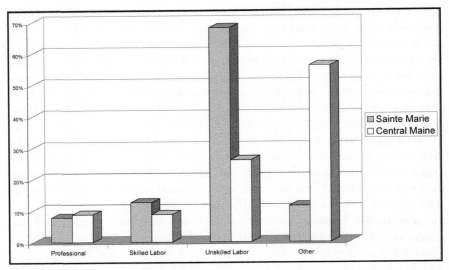

Figure 16: Comparison of Patient Occupations.

workers. As seen in Figure 16, patients who listed themselves as having a professional occupation represented 7.8 percent of all patients at Sainte-Marie compared to 8.8 percent at Central Maine. The percent of those classed as skilled laborers at Sainte-Marie was listed as 12.6 percent compared to 8.8 percent at Central Maine. The category of unskilled labor showed a much larger discrepancy between the two hospitals with 68.1 percent at Sainte-Marie and only 26.2 percent at Central Maine. As a percent of the total, Sainte-Marie served more than twice as many of the working class as Central Maine. These were the day laborers, mill workers, housekeepers, farmers and other menial workers of Lewiston and the surrounding area.

Central Maine General, on the other hand, had almost 13 percent more professionals as a percent of its patient population than Sainte-Marie. Central Maine's percent of patient occupations categorized as "Other" is extremely high at 56.1 percent compared to Sainte-Marie which recorded only 11.5 percent in the "Other" category. This difference is driven by the very high number of housewives and persons with no occupation reported by Central Maine. Sainte-Marie had no patients reported in either of these categories. These results seem to support the perception of Central Maine as the hospital of the establishment Yankees.

Since the Central Maine data was so weighted by the "Housewife" and "None" categories, a second analysis might be helpful in understanding if the general comparisons hold up. In this analysis, the "Housewife" and "None" categories were dropped out of the "Other" class at Central Maine. It was not necessary to do the same for the Sainte-Marie data, as mentioned prior no such occupations were reported. The patient occupation percentages for both hospitals were then recalculated. In this analysis, the unskilled labor percentage increases to about 44 percent of the total for Central Maine. However, this is still well below the 68 percent unskilled labor percentage reported for Sainte-Marie. Interestingly, while closing this gap slightly, the second analysis also increases the disparity between the two hospitals for the professional class percentage. This second analysis indicates that Sainte-Marie had 50 percent more unskilled labor patients (as a percent of the total) than Central Maine, and Central Maine had 50 percent more professional class patients than Sainte-Marie. These quantitative analyses, combined with the ethnicity data previously discussed, confirms the qualitative assessment of Sainte-Marie as the hospital of the working class and poor immigrant, and Central Maine as the hospital of the Yankee, whether elite or middle class.

Now that the ethnic and occupational background of each hospital's patients has been filled out to a certain extent, the nature of the complaints that led these patients to their respective hospitals will be examined. Data on medical conditions, causes of death, and patient financing (charitable care) was extracted from the annual reports for each hospital for each year between 1893 and 1908.

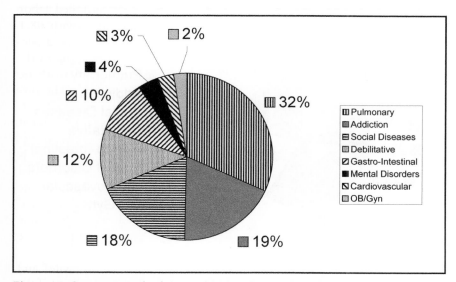

Figure 17: Common Medical Cases, Sainte-Marie, 1893–1908.

Figure 17 provides a summary classification of common medical cases for Sainte-Marie between 1893 and 1908.[7] Some of these classifications may be arguable due to medical terminology used to identify conditions prior to our contemporary diagnostic skills, but this analysis does provide a good picture of the ailments presented by Sainte-Marie's patients admitted to the hospital's medical department during the period of analysis. Almost one-third of the cases involved pulmonary complaints. However, the most common single medical condition treated at Sainte-Marie was alcohol addiction, which accounted for 405 cases between 1893 and 1908.[8]

Figure 18 provides the common medical cases for Central Maine General.[9] Unlike Sainte-Marie, alcohol addiction was a relatively minor complaint at Central Maine.[10] In addition, pulmonary complaints occurred at one-half the frequency as at Sainte-Marie. Both of these differences could be related to the socio-economic status of the different patient groups. Lewiston's Yankee elite would have lived and worked in cleaner environments than the textile and wage laborer living in Petit Canada and the neighborhoods around the mills. Moreover, several of Lewiston's largest Protestant congregations, such as the Baptists, Free Baptists and Methodists, did not encourage drinking. And finally the consumption of alcohol was often used to dull the grueling experiences that were everyday occurrences for most of the Sainte-Marie's wage-labor patients. However, Central Maine treated nine cases of opium addiction, while Sainte-Marie encountered none during this time; suggesting

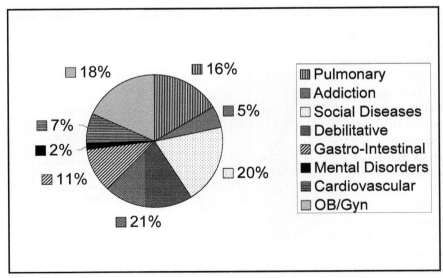

Figure 18: Common Medical Cases, Central Maine General, 1893–1908.

socio-economic differences in the drug of choice.[11] It is also possible that the wealthier inhabitants of the Lewiston area sought care for their addictions elsewhere, in order to protect their privacy. This same theory might account for the greater frequency of mental conditions presented at Sainte-Marie, about twice that for Central Maine.

It is also interesting to compare the prevalence of complaints in light of the ethnic and socioeconomic information previously provided. For example, Central Maine had enough married female patients to record a class of occupation as "housewife" and obstetrical and gynecological complaints were the third most prevalent category at that hospital. The working poor's hospital, Sainte-Marie, had no such occupational class recorded and such complaints were nine times less common than at Central Maine. To suggest that the immigrant women who filled Saints Pierre and Paul Church on Sunday were healthier than their Yankee counterparts is ludicrous; it is much more likely that these French-Canadian women felt that they had other obligations to discharge that took priority. The gender mortality differences at Sainte-Marie would also support this assumption. As seen later, due to the generosity of the Grey Nuns, the cost of medical care was one barrier that these women did not have to face, so this difference must be due to other factors, such as fear of losing a job, or one's family. Another category of common cases were cardiac-related conditions. In this instance, the more affluent Yankees at Central Maine presented these conditions more than twice as often as the poorer inhabitants of Petit Canada.

It is also instructive to see which complaints were presented in roughly the same frequency between the two hospitals. Complaints that could be classed within the loose (and admittedly euphemistically labeled) category of social diseases seemed to have been presented in roughly the same frequency. In fact, syphilis and gonorrhea accounted for 1.7 percent of the cases at Sainte-Marie and 1.9 percent of the cases at Central Maine over this time— sex as the great leveler, indeed. On a less lurid note, gastro-intestinal complaints also occurred in the same frequency at both hospitals, illustrating that dyspepsia (3.8 percent of all cases at Sainte-Marie and 4 percent of all cases at Central Maine) knows no socioeconomic or ethnic boundaries.

Urban life in the late nineteenth and early twentieth centuries, while much less uncertain than earlier rural colonial times, still represented a greater degree of risk and uncertainty than our relatively safe times. Medical conditions or surgical procedures that are relatively mild or routine in contemporary health care institutions were still dangerous in 1900, if not almost certainly fatal. Figure 19 provides a comparison of causes of death at Sainte-Marie and Central Maine for the period from 1893 to 1908.[12]

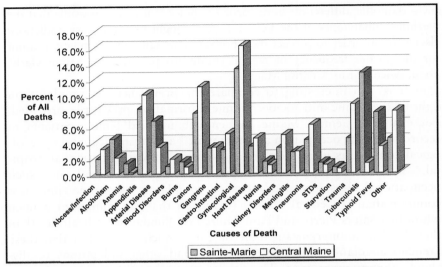

Figure 19: Common Causes of Death at Lewiston Hospitals, 1893–1908.

This data provides some interesting similarities and differences between the two hospitals and their patients. As cited previously, the number one cause of death at either hospital was complications from obstetrical or gynecological conditions. Clearly being a woman in the late nineteenth-century was medically dangerous to all, despite differences in either ethnic or economic status. However, remember that these complaints were nine times more common at Central Maine than at Sainte-Marie. Yet as a cause of mortality, these complaints were very similar; about 16 percent at Central Maine and 13 percent at Sainte-Marie. Another way of putting this is that complications from obstetrical or gynecological conditions were more than eight times as deadly for a patient at Sainte-Marie than for one at Central Maine. This may also account for the difference in gender mortality noted previously. It is sobering to realize that the immigrant women of Petit Canada needed to be at death's door before seeking medical care, in spite of the Grey Nuns' efforts at community outreach, which will further be described later.

Of the next four most frequent causes of death at these hospitals, two are the same, although their prevalence is different. The next four causes of death at Sainte-Marie were: tuberculosis, appendicitis, typhoid fever and cancer; while the next four at Central Maine were: cancer, appendicitis, trauma and "other." Even here the immigrant, working class status of Sainte-Marie's patients is apparent. A person dying at Sainte-Marie was more than twice as likely to die of typhoid fever then someone dying at Central Maine. The crowded, unsanitary living and working conditions of the French-Canadian immigrant laborer helped make this grisly statistic a reality. Even more compelling is the frequency of death from tuberculosis; which was almost ten times more common at Sainte-Marie than Central Maine. It is impossible to tell what effect Central Maine's policy of admitting "curable" patients may have had on these statistics. Of the other two most common causes of death, death from complications of appendicitis was relatively similar at both hospitals; while cancer, arguably at this date more commonly a fatal disease of the elderly and affluent, was about twice as likely to be the cause of death at Central Maine as opposed to Sainte-Marie. Death from trauma (typically blows sustained in accidents), was also about twice as common a cause of death at Central Maine versus Sainte-Marie.

Besides appendicitis, other similarly frequent causes of death included gangrene (about 3 percent at both hospitals) and hernia (about 1 percent at both). As for deaths from infectious agents, tuberculosis (lungs) and typhoid fever (intestinal organs), as discussed above, were more often causes of death for Sainte-Marie's patients. Pneumonia (lungs) was 50 percent more frequently a cause of death at Central Maine than at Sainte-Marie. Meningitis (brain lining) as a cause of death was found similarly at either hospital. Alcoholism, which was reported as a medical condition almost ten times more frequently for patients at Sainte-Marie as for those at Central Maine, was only twice as frequently a cause of death at Sainte-Marie than at Central Maine. Another way to look at this is deaths per reported cases treated. In this light, about one death from alcoholism per twenty reported cases was experienced at Sainte-Marie, while about one death from alcoholism per five reported cases was experienced at Central Maine.[13]

As shown by the compiled patient data from both institutions, the Grey Nuns served a patient population that was poorer, less educated, and subject to greater environmental stressors than the population that Central Maine General served, less than two miles away. The nuns' patients had more serious illnesses and fewer resiliencies than the patients at Central Maine General. Based on these facts, it would be expected that the sister-nurses would have a significant medical challenge in restoring their patients' health and discharging them as healthy. A review of the data, however, proves that the Grey Nuns, even with their open admission policy, were able to restore a comparable percent of patients to health, as compared to Central Maine General and its selective policy of only admitting the "curable" patients.

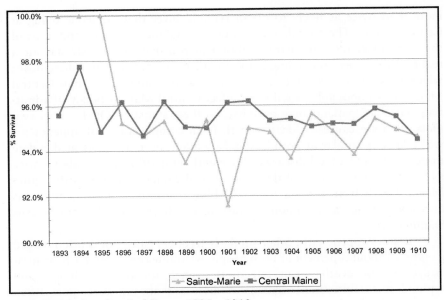

Figure 20: Patient Survival Rates, 1893—1910.

Figure 20 compares the annual patient survival rates for each hospital.[14] The data does show though that patient survival rate for Hospital General Sainte-Marie's was clearly more variable than at Central Maine General. The average survival rate for this period was 94.8 percent at Sainte-Marie compared to 95.5 percent at Central Maine.[15] While these averages are extremely close, the standard deviation for survival rate at Sainte-Marie was nearly three times that for Central Maine.[16] This variability is not surprising given the more difficult circumstances and patient complaints faced by the Grey Nuns, as discussed earlier. Given the mission that they undertook, the Grey Nuns delivered stellar care to their patients. Interestingly, the general trend for survival rate at both hospitals declined over the period under study. This probably represents several other trends in health care converging in this fact. For example, there was growing cultural acceptance in the general population of seeking hospital care for illness at this time. Institutional hygiene was improving, as well as the ability to safely transport patients to Lewiston's hospitals with the local trolley system. It is also possible that the injured were moved more quickly to hospitals, allowing them to die in the hospital instead of the mills or in their homes. Finally, perhaps the most telling comparative statistic is that the survival rates for both hospitals began to converge by 1903 and was very close for the last three years reviewed. Arguably this occurred due to the

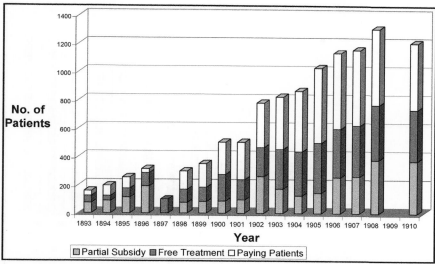

Figure 21: Charity Care, Sainte-Marie 1893–1910.

increasing professionalism of the sister-nurses and their success in raising funds for their hospital to improve the quality and depth of their medical service. This is borne out by the expanding lists of donations and physicians who practiced in the hospital as detailed by the Grey Nuns in their annual reports.

Not only did the sister-nurses face a patient population that had more difficult lives, they had to provide their nursing care to a population that could ill afford to pay for the medical treatment that they required. Figure 21 illustrates the growth in patient population for Sainte-Marie, subdivided by the status of patient payment.[17] For 16 of the 18 years, the number of patients who were either partially or completely subsidized by the Grey Nuns exceeded the number who paid for their care. In the other two years, the percent who paid was 52 percent to the 48 percent who were subsidized. In fact, Figure 23 clearly illustrates that the majority of the care provided by the sisters throughout this period was charitable and without full recompense. Given the widespread nature of subsidized medical treatment provided at the sisters' hospital, it is difficult to see how cost could be considered a barrier to those seeking treatment in Lewiston at this time.

In contrast, Central Maine General had a different theory of care and charity. This is dramatically revealed in Figure 22.[18] Throughout the fourteen-year period but especially between 1901 through 1907, the Central Maine General Hospital's Board of Directors and Superintendent both complained about the drain on their resources presented by patients needing

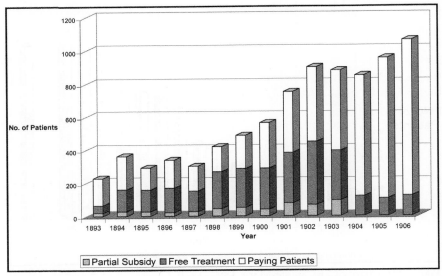

Figure 22: Charity Care, Central Maine General, 1893–1906.

wholly or partially subsidized treatment. For the three years prior to 1904, about 48 percent of Central Maine's patients were subsidized in some way. In 1904 the number of charity cases admitted to Central Maine dropped by more than two-thirds, and the hospital began to report just a total number of subsidized patients.[19] Superintendent William F. Smith reported in 1905 that it: " . . . is better understood [that state support] . . . is not with the idea that cities and towns have the right to cast the burden of caring for their own sick and indigent people upon the hospital."[20] The following year the continued presence of charity cases led Smith to demand that "some action be taken in the matter by the Officers of this hospital."[21] Apparently some action was taken by Central Maine directors, for in the 1907 Annual Report charity cases were not reported. What this action precisely was remains unknown. In several annual reports prior to 1907, reference is made to implementing strategies to reduce the number of patients who would need, or would ask, for charity. The rationale for such a decision by Central Maine was that "it is impossible for us to increase the number of charity patients unless we are provided with additional financial support."[22]

Hospital General Sainte-Marie was never the recipient of significant economic or medical aid as compared with Central Maine General Hospital. In fact, the number of charity cases at Sainte-Marie continued to grow after 1906, seemingly by another 10 percent after Central Maine's decision to restrict charity cases.[23] Yet Lewiston's community of Grey Nuns nevertheless prospered in this highly charged benevolent health care environment. Moreover they succeeded at protecting their separate identity as a community of French Canadian women religious who lived at, worked in and owned an American hospital. Initially met with hostility from Lewiston's elite Yankee community, their charism as sister-nurses to the suffering, the poor, and the Catholic, became an integral and valued element in the practice of health care in nineteenth and twentieth-century Lewiston.

Chapter Nine
Beyond Health Care

EDUCATION

Sheltering the poor and nursing the ill were paramount to the Grey Nuns, as witnessed by the dynamic expansion of their health care facilities. However, like the Catholic hierarchy, they realized that the survival of a non-English speaking immigrant community was as dependent upon their comprehension of the English language as their health. French Canadians were no exception. A bilingual school had to be established in Lewiston. As discussed, the Grey Nuns willingly accepted the alteration to their nursing ministry to include educational endeavors. This was necessary if they were to aggressively alter the plight of the poor, French Canadian wage-laborers, and children. Lewiston's political elite openly recognized their failure to provide primary education for the children of their city's working poor. As early as 1871, Lewiston's mayor addressed this failure in a desperate call for a solution in the City's Eighth Annual Report. In his address this official claimed that: "There were no less than 1741 scholars in this city whose names have not been registered in any grade of our schools, and a very considerable proportion of whom undoubtedly are destitute of even the simplest rudiments of education. Of the whole number of scholars in the city, 4316, the average attendance was only 1497."[1]

The mayor lamented that Lewiston only had a 34 percent attendance rate in its schools, even though, "[w]e have a law upon our statute books requiring the attendance of every scholar under the age of fifteen years employed in our mills, at least three months in every year." He admitted that this law was a "dead letter," and then proceeded to end his address by answering his own questions: "[w]e must bear in mind that by far the largest proportion of these scholars are children of the poor, and that their labor, in the mills, or elsewhere, is absolutely essential to keep the wolf from the door,—that without that labor starvation or the poor-house would be the fate of many a family."[2]

The lack of consistent attendance by French Canadian children within Lewiston's primary public and parochial schools was due to several reasons. Many French Canadian families lived in extreme poverty, especially when they first immigrated to Lewiston. Both the earning power of children and their help in domestic arrangements was required if the family was to survive in their new environment.[3] Secondly, Protestant Christianity was pervasive in the educational agenda of Lewiston's public schools, which as discussed previously, French Canadians found unacceptable. And finally, the lack of English skills among the newly immigrated French Canadians prohibited children from attending any non-bilingual schools. Of course, no such school existed in Yankee-dominated Lewiston at this time.

Twenty years before Lewiston's mayor delivered his address, the publishers of the *Catholic Almanac* recognized the need to establish primary schools to educate Catholic children:

> "The wide-spread heresy of our land, and its vast efforts of propaganda[ism], the mixture of Catholics with Protestants, especially in parts seldom visited by a priest, the growing materialism of the age, which imperceptibly but effectually weans the heart from the spiritual objects of faith, are causes that still operate largely to the disadvantage of religion, and call for the most vigorous measures to oppose their influence. These will be found in the continual accession of pious and learned clergymen to the field of the ministry, in the spiritual retreats for the clergy and laity that are so effectual in renovating the life of the soul, and in the establishment of Catholic schools, under the charge of religious orders or congregations, for the imparting of a solid and virtuous education, and in various other means which the wisdom of the bishops has adopted."[4]

Catholic schools, however, had to function within the educational and financial limitations of the expanding poor and immigrant population that needed the labor of their children to survive. Moreover they existed in opposition to the Protestant American culture, which required the reading of the King James Bible in public schools. As Laura Offenhartz Greene points out, one of the central concerns of the Protestant reformers was not the working conditions of children but their lack of formal education: "illiterates could not read the Bible."[5] While Protestant reformers and the Catholic hierarchy disagreed over which version of the Bible to read, they were in agreement, however, over the critical role education plays in the American political system. By the time of the Third Plenary Council of Baltimore, November 8,

Figure 23: Students of L'Ecole Notre Dame, the First Bilingual School in Maine, 1883.

1884, American archbishops, bishops, abbots and superiors of religious orders would decree that "every parish was to have a school within two years of the council unless the bishops judged otherwise."[6]

As Catholic schools became viable institutions they were placed under the domain of church authority, not secular. Hence religious communities were now highly valued as religious educators that protected the Catholic faith while also instructing immigrant children how to adapt to the American culture. Even when teaching was not their primary calling, sisters such as the Grey Nuns nevertheless became educators of the immigrant poor. Preceding the educational decree of the Third Plenary Council by six years, the Grey Nuns founded a parochial school three weeks after their arrival in Lewiston. On November 21, 1878, L'Ecole de Notre Dame de Lourdes (the School of Our Lady of Lourdes) opened its doors.[7] This school represented the first bilingual educational institution in the State of Maine.[8] Unfortunately, no evidence has survived on the curriculum taught by the Grey Nuns at L'Ecole Notre Dame. But according to documents in the Portland Diocesan Chancery, the French language remained the predominant language in all Lewiston parochial schools, except in the Anglophone Saint Joseph and Wallace schools, until after World War One.[9]

Both the parish records of the French Canadian national church of Saint Pierre and the Grey Nuns' chronicle document that school attendance exceeded 200 students in the first year of L'Ecole Notre Dame.[10] In addition to parochial education the need for English skills among French Canadian adults had to be addressed. The demanding schedule of the textile mills and domestic responsibilities prohibited participation in day academies. The Grey Nuns responded to the needs of the adult women for academic instruction and opened an evening school for eighty young French Canadian women on February 26, 1879.[11] The annals recorded that the demands of these two schools, in addition to ongoing nursing of the ill, caused the sisters "extreme exhaustion."[12] While the evening school had to be discontinued within the year, the sisters continued to offer private language lessons and tutoring to young women, which was a common practice among foreign communities of women religious. For example, the Grey Nuns received an annual fee of $8.00 for tutoring one Mademoiselle Caron in French during 1894. The fees collected from these lessons represented a primary source of income for the Grey Nuns, especially during the formative years of the community.[13]

Despite the closure of their adult evening school, the Grey Nuns were rapidly emerging as leaders in education and child care. The community and their endeavors received financial support from a local group of Catholic French Canadian women, the Association of the Ladies of Charity, established in 1879.[14] This charitable organization's expressed purpose was to "second the efforts of the Sisters of Charity in their work with the poor and the sick and to help payoff the enormous debt which the sisters had incurred."[15] The supportive relationship between these two distinct groups of women, one religious and the other lay, has continued, with minor modifications, until the present day.

The Grey Nuns recorded their credits and expenses in an accounting journal. Similarly to the annals, the information recorded in the journal was dependent upon the prerogative of the sister accountant. Despite the lack of uniformity by the sister-accountants, the Grey Nuns' journal does contain the most accurate information that has survived on their fiscal activities. In this document, the order recorded that the monetary amounts raised from bazaars and raffles by the Ladies of Charity were an essential source of income for the sisters. In 1884, the donation by this organization of $141.39 represented the largest monetary contribution for that year.[16]

In addition to the support of the Ladies of Charity, the Grey Nuns also received financial compensation from the Dominican fathers for their services as teachers in the Dominican Block's parochial school. The five-story brick building was located at the corner of Lincoln and Chestnut Streets in Lewiston's Petit Canada. While nearly abandoned today, the Dominican Block building still stands, just down the street from the abandoned Grand Trunk Railway ticket office. The Dominican Block functioned as a French Canadian community center where both educational and social activities operated. When the facility opened in 1883, nine Grey Nuns served as teachers to 700 children. In January, 1883, the Saint-Hyacinthe Superior General visited the Lewiston community of Grey Nuns and wrote the following account of their teaching ministry: "I am satisfied with my visits to the classrooms, which seem to have taken off on a good foot and [are] frequented by a great amount of students. The teachers seem to be filled with devotion and desire to have the children advance and to give them all a knowledge and love of our holy religion."[17]

In 1886 the Grey Nuns' teaching responsibilities at the Dominican Block were lessened when a religious order of Brothers from Lyons France, The Little Brothers of Marist, commonly known as the Marist Brothers, arrived in Lewiston. The Marist Brothers assumed the educational responsibility for the French Canadian boys in the upper grades at the Dominican Block. The Grey Nuns were ultimately released of all teaching responsibilities at the Dominican Block when the Sisters of Sion arrived in Lewiston and Auburn from Canada in 1892.

CHILD CARE

It was in the field of providing child care that the Grey Nuns of Lewiston demonstrated their inclusive understanding of what welfare institutions, in addition to hospitals, are necessary to foster a health society. Both orphanages also provided a pragmatic but essential social service to Lewiston's working poor. The demands required from those who worked in Lewiston's textile mills were both physical and psychological. In the Lewiston mill complex, the weekday shift ran from 6 A.M. to 7 P.M. with a forty-five minute dinner break from 12 to 12:45. Saturday's schedule started at 6 A.M., stopping at noon or extending to 6:30 P.M.[18] Furthermore child labor laws and protective services did not exist in nineteenth-century America. In Lewiston, entire French Canadian families were often employed by the mills regardless of sex and age of the family members "to keep the wolf from the door."[19] Verification of the employment of children in Lewiston's mills, however, is difficult due to the accounting methods used by the mill overseers. In the Libby Mill ledger, there is no indication or distinction if the employee is an adult or a child. The pay ratio is indicative of some discrimination between laborers, but the basis for this accounting can only be

Figure 24: Spool Room employees, Bates Mill, 1895.

speculated. As recorded in one particular ledger, there were three laborers with the last name of Roy employed by the mill, who all worked together in the same carding room. They were Valerie Roy and Valida Roy who were paid the same rate of 2 and 3/8ths but Rose Anna Roy was paid at a lower rate of 1 and 7/8ths rate.[20]

According to a previous study, an estimated 91 percent of French Canadian children, ranging in age from ten to sixteen years, labored in either Lewiston or Auburn mills by 1870.[21] The employment of children in the textile industry was a long standing tradition among French Canadian families which "gave rise to serious abuses in many instances."[22] The Rhode Island Census of 1875 reported that 64 percent of French Canadian children between the ages of five to fourteen worked in that state; children ten years or younger comprising 20 percent of this figure by 1875.[23]

The Grey Nuns' annals recorded that Demerise Charest was the first child placed with the sisters in June of 1879, only seven months after the sisters' arrival from Saint-Hyacinthe.[24] By 1883 the sisters provided ongoing care, both long and short term, for thirteen children.[25] Children were left in the care of the sisters for a few days, weeks, or months. Children were also dropped off on a daily basis when other domestic arrangements could not be secured. Child care services provided a small but valuable source of income for the sisters when a parent could make a donation for their child's care. Although these children were identified in the chronicle as orphans, the fluidity of their movement in the Grey Nun's care is indicative that they had families and other sources of care. The orphanage would remain a central part of the Grey Nuns' social service organization until it was closed in June 1971. Until 1888 all of the girls lived with the sisters, occupying the same tiny domain on Pierce and Walnut Streets and then the Golder House. They were eventually relocated to a house on the corner of Orange, Pine and Sabattus Streets.[26]

The lack of space in the sisters' tiny convent created intimate living conditions that prevented the luxury of class distinctions among the children, while also making a strict religious atmosphere for the sisters impossible. Yet the limited confines of the Grey Nuns' convent also fostered a sense of community, even family, among the children and sisters; a heritage that remains warmly remembered by the descendants of those who were welcomed into the Grey Nuns' home.

The practice of women religious communities sharing their private living space with orphans, boarders, and students until separate accommodations could be constructed was not unusual among immigrant communities. This practice was particularly common during a new community's founding period when resources were scarce and the order's living condi-

Figure 25: One of the Grey Nuns' Charges.

tions were tentative. The Sisters of St. Joseph of Carondelet in their first convent in Missouri, like the Grey Nuns shared their limited space with children who had been entrusted to the sisters' care. According to witnesses these sisters displayed affectionate and encouraging behavior towards the children in their convent. In both communities the boarders and sisters took "recreation" together and shared in income-making activities.[27]

The Grey Nuns and the children entrusted to their care all lived as a single community; all children were recorded in the institution's records, the Grey Nuns' summary, as "orphan." Yet use of the term "orphan" to designate the children's status was not accurate. In reality the children living with the Grey Nuns came from a variety of domestic situations with the minority having two deceased parents.

Surviving records show that many of the children who were placed in the sisters' care had at least one living parent or relative that paid for expenses. As stated in the *1908 Annual Report of the Girls' Orphanage,* "while a large number [orphans] are received gratuitously [a] few of the children have their board paid by relatives."[28] These children usually stayed less than five years with the sisters. If multiple siblings were placed in the orphanage their departure dates consistently coincided. One can reasonably conclude that the majority of children in the sister's care returned home to their primary family during the year or were relocated to relatives in New England or Quebec.[29]

As mentioned previously, the percentage of children either cited in the registry as "O" for orphan or listed with both parents deceased comprised a minority, even though all children were identified by the sisters as orphans. The Grey Nuns never limited their outreach to only parentless children. In actuality the Grey Nuns' "orphanage" was a place of refuge for the burdened wage-labor parent, or a facility that provided care to children whose parents required assistance. The *1908 Annual Report of the Girls' Orphanage* disclosed that of the 115 girls who had lived in the orphanage during the year, 24 children (20 percent) paid full board, 40 children (34 percent) paid partial board, while 51 children (44 percent) received free care.[30] Furthermore the sisters' orphanage also functioned as an inclusive child care facility which was open to any Catholic and non-Catholic child regardless of their ethnic heritage or place of birth. As indicated by the baptismal records cited in the registry, several children placed with the sisters had received a Catholic baptism in Ireland.[31] The *1908 Annual Report of the Girls' Orphanage,* listed the United States, Canada, and Nova Scotia as places of birth for the children in 1908. The report also recorded that the girls in the sisters' care came from fifteen different Maine cities and towns.[32]

In addition to the girls' orphanage, the Grey Nuns founded a separate institution on September 4, 1893 to provide similar care for young boys. The land for this institution had been purchased by the sisters from the Franklin Company for $12,500 twelve years prior to the founding of the institution.[33] The Healy Asylum, named after the most Reverend Bishop James A. Healy, would provide child care services in Lewiston for eighty years until its closure on July 1, 1973. "The principal aim of this institution," the Grey Nuns declared in the 1896 Annual Report, "is to provide a home for little boys, who have been left orphans, or who have been forsaken by their parents, thus enabling them, by instruction and advice, to become, later on, honest and respectable citizens."[34]

Within three years of its founding, the Healy Asylum had provided care to over two hundred boys ranging in age from two to twelve years and from various domestic situations. These children cited their nationalities as Americans, Canadians, Scottish and English. The largest percentage was born in the United States with families residing in Maine, Massachusetts, and New Hampshire.[35] There was a higher percentage of ethnic diversity in the Healy Asylum compared to the girls' orphanage. A possible reason for this was that the Healy Asylum was closely connected to the Portland chancery and regularly received boys for placement from the greater Portland area.

The Healy Asylum operated as a structurally distinct institution separate from the Grey Nuns' welfare and medical complex of Hospital General Sainte-Marie. It was located on Ash Street, approximately one mile from the hospital and the girls' orphanage. Unlike the girls' orphanage, the Healy Asylum was run autonomously under the authority of a separately appointed Grey Nun Superior. Furthermore the Healy Asylum had the additional objective of reforming boys who had committed legal transgressions, as stated in their 1896 Annual Report:

> "One of the Objectives of this institution is to aid, advise and encourage to lead a better life, such boys as have thoughtlessly or intentionally, been guilty of some petty offence whereby they have become amenable to the law. Owing to the kindness of the presiding magistrates, the sisters, for the last few years, have been allowed to take charge of several young boys, guilty of some misdemeanor."[36]

The Grey Nuns' obligation to reform juvenile boys in addition to maintaining the Healy Asylum's educational and care standards for all the children taxed the sisters' limited economic resources.[37] This contributed to a strain between the Grey Nuns and Portland diocesan authorities who minimally supported Healy Asylum services for the boys whom they sent to the sisters. Unlike the girls' orphanage, the Healy Asylum did not receive the indirect benefit of the institutional expansion of the Asylum of Our Lady of Lourdes. In the Portland chancery archives, a two-year correspondence between Sister Dion, the Superior of the Healy Asylum, and Reverend Denis J. O'Brien, the Rector of the Cathedral in Portland, detailed the constant tension between the Grey Nuns' desire to provide care and education to the boys in their care and the fiscal reality that too often forced difficult decisions.

An example of this conflict was played out in the fate of the Britting children. Sister Dion wrote to Reverend O'Brien on March 20, 1900: "I shall take this opportunity to remind you of what I shall have to do with the Britting children that you asked me to keep a few more days when you came to visit the orphanage. If you do not give me other instructions *by a letter from you* I shall *consider them here at your expense* [emphasis in original]."[38]

Sister Dion's harsh and judgmental tone, however, was not a reflection upon the Britting children's poverty, but rather on O'Brien's continual failure to fulfill his economic obligations to the orphanage. In a cry of frustration Sister Dion had written earlier in the same letter, over another monetary issue, that "whether it [the bill] will be paid by you personally or by the Fathers matters little so long as it is paid. The difficulty exists with the principle."[39]

By March 30th the unfortunate situation of the Britting children was resolved by O'Brien. While O'Brien's letter to Sister Dion has not survived, one can assume from her response on March 30, 1900 that O'Brien failed to secure financial support for the Britting children and they were separated from their father. On that day, Sister Dion wrote:

> "After having received your letter, I addressed myself to the City of Lewiston to send the Britting children back to Portland without putting them out in the street. The Overseer of the Poor of Lewiston notified the Overseer in Portland to kindly take care of these children. He responded yesterday that he would accept them and that they should be sent to him immediately. They left this morning, accompanied by a Police Officer."[40]

As this letter testifies it was Sister Dion not O'Brien, who prevented the Britting children from homelessness while arranging protection for their travel to Portland. She concluded the letter with a request that O'Brien take action on behalf of the Britting children: "I wanted to alert you to this so you could keep it in mind, if you think it best, if they are going to be placed."[40] The request was written in the humblest of language, which was common in correspondence between women religious and the male hierarchy. To work and mission within the male controlled power structures of the Catholic Church, women religious knew that they had to master the art of humble diplomacy if they were to achieve their objectives.

By July Sister Dion's tactical handling of O'Brien had resulted in success. She had achieved her monetary objective for the Asylum, made O'Brien financially accountable for the children, and had gained the return of two of the Britting children from Portland. In a letter to O'Brien dated July 9, 1900, Dion wrote: "Please accept my sincere thanks for your check, it could not have arrived at a more opportune time. I would willingly accept the two Britting children, but it is impossible for me to take Johnnie into the Orphanage at age 14, and since he cannot work in the factories, we cannot take him in."[42]

Sister Dion, however, did accept Johnnie Britting into the Healy Asylum where he remained until June of 1901. The rationale for Dion's acceptance of Johnnie Britting is unknown. There is some surviving evidence that the child may have been either physically or mentally handicapped. In a letter to O'Brien, dated November 23, 1900, Dion does mention that the Asylum had "received a letter from Mr. Alfred Britting, with money for his children's expenses."[43] Nevertheless, by June 1901 Johnnie Britting was returned to an older brother who resided in Portland. Sister Dion explained her decision in a letter to O'Brien: "This child, whom the pastor already feels I have kept too long, is more than 15 years old and is not intelligent enough for us to put to work in the factory since the danger of accidents is so great. So I am obliged, by my own principle, to send him away." Yet Dion concludes this letter with an appeal to O'Brien "in case you have other views on Johnnie, and if so, please let me know this week."[44]

The details of the Britting family's domestic situation are unknown, but the consequences were not unique. Homelessness, abandonment, and dependency characterized the marginal life of the class of immigrant wage laborers. When a nineteenth-century immigrant Catholic family encountered economic difficulties, emotional upheaval, illness or mental and physical abuse they often turned for aid to their faith community. This reliance on the institutional Church at times of domestic crisis was detailed in a correspondence between O'Brien and Dion over the return of a child to his mother who was in her care:

> "I just received a letter from Mrs. Thomas . . . asking me what day our classes end, because she says she has returned home, her husband having decided to behave better, as well as herself (I do not know all of the details). And she would like to come get her boy Tommy. Seeing as you entrusted the child with us, I did not want to send him back without your consent."[45]

Catholic immigrants thus acknowledged the church and clergy's role and authority in both the spiritual and corporal realms of their lives. This acknowledgement of Church authority however must not be confused with meek acquiescence. The explosive confrontation between the laity and Church hierarchy that has marked every century of United States history, is ample testimony to the laity's ability to distinguish between respect for position and the right to question authority in public when necessary. The Maine corporation sole controversy of 1911 is one such example.[46]

The Grey Nuns, however, did not belong to the Catholic elite. Rather they were perceived by the laity, who desperately needed welfare assistance and health care, as the caring daughters of a mothering church. As sister-nurses, the Grey Nuns understood the physical limitations of human life; as nineteenth-century women they understood that domesticity was a cruel taskmaster; and as vowed women they intimately understood the beauty of the human soul. The Grey Nuns combined their knowledge of the world in which they dwelled and their aggressive spirituality which in turned trans-formed their Catholic identity as caregivers. The feminist scholar Maria Harris has argued that women who become: "[c]are givers are taught about human relations through their caring—about the body's frailty, about the suddenness with which life's circumstance change.... Caretakers have fewer illusions about the two greatest religious realities—-birth and death—than those who have not been schooled by Care."[47]

In conclusion, the Grey Nuns' religious self understanding as care-givers led them to embrace the children and women of Lewiston who required domestic aid and physical care. Their response was to turn their convent into a surrogate home to the children and a hospice to the suffering ill. In contemporary terms, the sisters' convent was the equivalent to a multi-care facility. It was a day-care center, an assisted living facility for the elderly, and a hospice for critically ill children and their families. By estab-lishing an orphanage that was not limited to parentless children and that was run with an open-door policy, the Grey Nuns created a flexible institu-tion that was directed to the particular needs of Lewiston's immigrants and working poor that effectively addressed the turbulent stages of an industri-alizing community.

Conclusion

The Grey Nuns' community in Lewiston continually re-crafted their care giving and nursing skills to mitigate the suffering of the ill and the poor. The Grey Nuns as vowed women were spiritually motivated and their goals were religious, yet they never lost the importance of material provision that is tied to the profession of nursing. [1]

As skilled adaptors, the Grey Nuns recognized the scientific and professional advancements in medical care and responded accordingly. Their behavior contributed to both their success as sister-nurses and the survival of their hospital. As detailed in their registry, prior to their formal incorporation as a hospital in 1892, the Grey Nuns were sufficiently adept at nursing that they could provide medical care to an ethnically diverse population. Their legal act of incorporation was an "exercise of power." As Michel Foucault has accurately written, "in western societies since the Middle Ages, the exercise of power has always been formulated in terms of law."[2]

Furthermore despite their demanding work, the Lewiston community of Grey Nuns and their institutions prospered.[3] Hospital General Sainte-Marie's close connection to issues surrounding women's health led, nearly a hundred years later, to the establishment of a pro-active women's health care facility. The center was built close to the site where Jeanne Montez Carpentier died. The motto selected by this facility to promote women's health is: "Take care of yourself and all else will follow." The Grey Nuns knew the harsh truth of these words not only in the lives of the women they nursed, but in their own. They put this knowledge into action and built a hospital and two orphanages that focused on the complex needs of women, children and wage-labor dependent families.

While successful at adaptation, the Grey Nuns were not radical women in their feminist religiosity. Both as care givers and institution

Figure 26: The Grey Nuns Serving at their Own Hospital Function.

builders, the Grey Nuns always contextualized their health care ministries in accordance with the tenets of their Catholic faith. To do this in a faith that was paternalistic, hierarchical, and authoritarian required specific skills. Public and private diplomacy was a skill which the Grey Nuns mastered in Lewiston. This was revealed by the behavior of the community's Superiors in letters and invitations to diocesan authority to bless their hospital foundations or approve their endeavors.[4] When in the presence of Church or professional medical authorities, the sisters would defer self-recognition. At both public dedications of their hospitals, it was the Bishop Healy and then O'Connell who received both monetary compensation and community appreciation for the foundations, not the Grey Nuns.[5]

As their behavior and works testified, the Grey Nuns' ministry was open, inclusive, and outwardly focused. Their actions were the manifestation of a spirituality exercised for more than a hundred years. Being seen by both the Church and the public as non-threatening members of the community, the Grey Nuns were able to secure their religious identity and right to minister to the suffering and poor, as they determined.

Thus the communal story of the Grey Nuns and in particular the story of Sister Mary of the Incarnation, are stories of achievement. These women had achieved what a century later would be termed "self-actualization." This accomplishment was made all the more significant in view of the fact that the order lived in a hostile, foreign, Protestant-dominated, industrial environment while submerged in a Catholic world of ethnicity, traditions and paternalism. This environment had demanded that the sisters learn new urban life skills while they tried to maintain their ethno-religious identity as a community of Catholic French Canadian sister-nurses. But it was precisely their identity as Grey Nuns, which may seem to the modern sensibility as a radical surrendering of self that ultimately gave the sisters the necessary abilities to balance these different claims in a very different reality for them and yet succeed memorably.

Appendix A
Lewiston's Parish Statistics

The systematic preservation of historical religious records from the nineteenth century is problematic. Many Catholic parishes and diocesan records of this era, in the rural nineteenth century Portland Diocese in general and Lewiston parishes in particular, can be spotty and even sometimes contradictory. This problem, at time, affects this study.

Many parish pastors, furthermore, were not accountants, and even had problems accurately counting their own parishioners. This accounts for some of the discrepancies apparent in the parish statistics. At least one pastor, Reverend Wallace of Saint Joseph's parish in Lewiston, submitted his statistical report for the year (1877) twice, each time with slightly different numbers. In addition, parish and diocesan records were also lost or damaged through neglect or fire. Bishop James Healy's note from 1875, reproduced below, attests to the disruption fire could have on current diocesan business, much less posterity.

Lewiston. Me

Portland, June 2d. 1875.

Rev and Dear Sir :

      You are perhaps aware that in the great conflagration of 1866, many valuable Diocesan papers were destroyed. I am: therefore, compelled to request a speedy answer to the following questions, in order to know the state of the diocese.

      Write the answer on this paper and transmit to me without fail by July 1st, 1875.

      Yours faithfully in Christ,

      † *James A. Healy,*

         Bishop of Portland.

Bishop James Healy's 1875 Letter on Loss of Diocesan Records[1]

Table 1. Saints Pierre & Paul Parish, 1876–1899[2]

Year	Catholics	Baptisms	Parish Population	Families	Family Size	Marriages
1876	3000	164	3164	472	6.7	43
1877	3074	144	3218	500	6.4	35
1878	3500	181	3681	600	6.1	54
1879	4000	168	4168	660	6.3	58
1880	5000	233	5233	750	7.0	54
1881		228	228			
1882	6000	262	6262	1000	6.3	78
1883	6000	260	6260	1000	6.3	103
1884	6800	330	7130	1200	5.9	90
1885	7500	316	7816	1500	5.2	71
1886						
1887	6500	348	6848	1500	4.6	87
1888	7550	370	7920			85
1889	8000	387	8387	1700	4.9	89
1890	8500	429	8929	1700	5.3	105
1891	9880	501	10381			96
1892	10000	477	10477			120
1893	10690	504	11194			119
1894	9785	507	10292			94
1895	10660	529	11189			109
1896	11000	574	11574			108
1897	11000	521	11521			96
1898	11500	496	11996			95
1899	11500	482	11982			107

Table 2. Saint Joseph Parish, 1873–1899[3]

Year	Catholics	Baptisms	Parish Population	Families	Family Size	Marriages
1873	4000	113	4113			16
1874						
1875						
1876	5000	135	5135			34
1877	3000	148	3148	640	4.9	20
1878	3200	156	3356	630	5.3	36
1879						
1880	3800	138	3938	670	5.9	36
1881	3500	156	3656	640	5.7	33
1882	4000	126	4126	640	6.4	23
1883	4000	126	4126	680	6.1	26
1884						
1885	4000	130	4130	640	6.5	24
1886	4000	125	4125	630	6.5	18
1887	4000	113	4113	600	6.9	18
1888	4000	115	4115	600	6.9	22
1889	4000	108	4108	640	6.4	20
1890	4000	120	4120	630	6.5	30
1891	4000	130	4130	620	6.7	29
1892	4000	118	4118	600	6.9	30
1893	4200	134	4334	630	6.9	
1894	1550	5	1555	320	4.9	
1895	1600	45	1645	300	5.5	15
1896	1600	56	1656	312	5.3	16
1897	1600	44	1644	300	5.5	12
1898	1534	47	1581	312	5.1	12
1899	1649	51	1700	310	5.5	10

Table 3. Saint Patrick Parish, 1894–1899[4]

Year	Catholics	Baptisms	Parish Population	Families	Family Size	Marriages
1894	2200	124	2324	398	5.8	
1895	2200	76	2276	400	5.7	
1896	2000	89	2089	400	5.2	
1897	2200	72	2272	450	5.0	
1898	2200	86	2286	450	5.1	
1899	2300	77	2377	450	5.3	

Appendix B
Hospital General Sainte-Marie Patient Statistics[1]

Table 1. Hospital General Sainte-Marie Patient Survival Rates, 1893–1910

Year	Deceased Patients	Live Patients	Total Patients	Percent Survival
1893	0	160	160	100.0%
1894	0	198	198	100.0%
1895	0	256	256	100.0%
1896	15	300	315	95.2%
1897	17	301	318	94.7%
1898	14	285	299	95.3%
1899	21	302	323	93.5%
1900	21	433	454	95.4%
1901	46	503	549	91.6%
1902	41	781	822	95.0%
1903	45	824	869	94.8%
1904	55	816	871	93.7%
1905	47	1028	1075	95.6%
1906	71	1134	1205	94.9%
1907	76	1156	1232	93.8%
1908	63	1307	1370	95.4%
1909	65	1212	1277	94.9%
1910	69	1206	1275	94.6%
Total	1893	12202	12868	94.8%

Table 2. Hospital General Sainte-Marie Subsidization of Patients, 1893–1910[2]

Year	Free Treatment	Partial Subsidy	Total Subsidized	Paying Patients	Total Patients
1893	50	75	125	35	160
1894	35	90	125	73	198
1895	63	115	178	78	256
1896	92	194	286	29	315
1897	118	81	199	119	318
1898	94	77	171	128	299
1899	102	84	186	166	352
1900	188	88	276	227	503
1901	143	97	240	263	503
1902	204	262	466	315	781
1903	278	176	454	370	824
1904	310	127	437	429	866
1905	352	147	499	529	1028
1906	341	257	598	536	1134
1907	359	263	622	534	1156
1908	388	380	768	539	1307
1909					
1910	363	372	735	471	1206
Total	3480	2885	6365	4841	11206

Table 3. Hospital General Sainte-Marie Patient Occupations, 1897–1900[3]

Year	Skilled Labor	Professionals	Unskilled Labor	Others
1897	9%	8.6%	76.7%	5.7%
1898	15.7%	6.7%	68.2%	9.4%
1899	12.5%	9.2%	66.8%	11.5%
1900	13.2%	6.7%	60.7%	19.4%

Table 4. Hospital General Sainte-Marie Common Medical Complaints, 1893–1908[4]

Condition	1893	1894	1895	1896	1897	1898	1899	1900	1901	1902	1903	1904	1905	1906	1907	1908	Total Cases
Abortion	1													3			3
Albuminaria													3				3
Addiction - Alcohol				1			9	12	8	28	30	23	51	54	82	107	405
Addiction - Morphine											3	1	5	3	4		16
Addiction - Opium																	
Anemia	12	11	11	13			4	12	2	27	5	9	6	1	6	4	123
Apoplexy							1	1	1	1							4
Asthma	5	3		2			1		6	3	4	2	3		2	3	34
Bronchitis	6	11	21	16			18	18	25	52	38	14	20	11	13	30	293
Cancer (all)	2		1				1	1			1	1		7	8	4	26
Cirrhosis of Liver	1			1			1		3	4	1	2	2		1		15
Cystitis			1	3			3	4	2		3	4	5	13	10	5	54
Delirium Tremens			6	1				4	2	11	3	16	5	1	3		52
Dementia									1	3	3	3	2	2			14
Diarrhea				17						5							22
Dysentery	1	1		1						5							8
Dyspepsia	8		8	1					5	15	3	14	5	6	16	11	92
Endometritus											9			4		3	16
Epilepsy		2					2	1		1	3	5	1			1	16
Exhaustion/Debility											1	7	2	3	4	12	29

(continued)

Table 4. Hospital General Sainte-Marie Common Medical Complaints, 1893–1908[4] (continued)

Condition	Year																Total Cases
	1893	1894	1895	1896	1897	1898	1899	1900	1901	1902	1903	1904	1905	1906	1907	1908	
Gastro-related				3			4	9	6	6	8	27	21	12	25	27	148
Hepatitis	6			3			2	12	5	3	7	5	5	5	4	1	58
Heart Disease (all)	5	3		1			3		2	8	6	8	12	5	8	14	75
Hypochondria										2	1	2	1				6
Hysteria							1	4		2	1		5		1	3	17
Influenza		5					9	2	10		8	3	5	2	29	32	105
Insanity							1	2	1		2	4	7	1	9	11	38
Melancholia		2	3	4			1	2	1	1	2	1	1				16
Mania										2	3				1		7
Measles			1				20	1						2	1		25
Menstrual Complications		12		1									1	1	4	2	21
Miscarriage														2	3	1	6
Nervous Prostration		7									1	2	1				11
Neuralgia			7						1		1	1	3		4		18
Neurasthenia		3		16			10	12		26	7	10	11	19	25	21	160
Obstetrics											2		2				4
Ovaritis	1										12				1	1	15
Pneumonia	10	5	4				4	10	19	20	34	10	23	34	30	19	222

(continued)

Table 4. Hospital General Sainte-Marie Common Medical Complaints, 1893–1908[4] (continued)

Condition	Year																Total Cases
	1893	1894	1895	1896	1897	1898	1899	1900	1901	1902	1903	1904	1905	1906	1907	1908	
Rheumatism (all)	7	12	3				5	8	9	21	8	13	17	37	34	32	206
Scrofula	7		4								1						12
Starvation											1	1	1	3	2		8
Syphilis/Gonorrhea		1					4	3	2		6			14	21	16	67
Tuberculosis	3		4				13	11	17	20	20	17	25	17	14	15	176
Typhoid Fever	25	6	15	25			24	32	31	10	16	45	56	26	10	14	335
Annual Cases	106	102	143	134			171	195	193	324	309	294	403	525	549	497	3945

Table 5. Hospital General Sainte-Marie Causes of Death, 1893-1908[5]

Condition	1893	1894	1895	1896	1897	1898	1899	1900	1901	1902	1903	1904	1905	1906	1907	1908	Total Cases
Abscess Or Infection		2	1				1	1			2	1	1	1			10
Alcoholism				1		3					1	2	4		5	7	23
Anemia				1				1		3	1		1				7
Appendicitis						1		1	2	1	4	2	6	8	6	12	43
Arterial Disease				3		1		2	1	3	6	2	5	1	8	3	35
Blood Disorders							1				1		1		1	1	5
Burns							1					2	1		2	2	8
Cancer	1	3	1				1	4	1	1	4	9	4	3	3	5	40
Gangrene		1	1	1							4	1	1	6	2		17
Gastro-Intestinal	2							1	1	1	1	4		2	3		16
Gynecological			3			3	3	6	4	7	2	9	5	9	11	7	69
Heart Disease		1	2						2	5		3	1		2	2	18
Hernia						1		1			2	1		1	1	2	8
Kidney Disorders									2	5	1	1	2	1	3	5	17
Meningitis				2					2	1	1	3	1		3	3	14
Pneumonia	2		1						1	2	4			2	2	4	22

(continued)

Table 5. Hospital General Sainte-Marie Causes of Death, 1893-1908[5] (continued)

Condition	Year																Total Cases
	1893	1894	1895	1896	1897	1898	1899	1900	1901	1902	1903	1904	1905	1906	1907	1908	
Syphilis									1					4	2		7
Starvation										1			1	1		1	4
Trauma				1		1	1			2	1	2	1	4	1	9	23
Tuberculosis	3	2	4			2	5	3	4	6	7	3	4	6	10	7	66
Typhoid Fever	2	3	2				7		1		2	6	3	6		7	40
Other				1		2	1	1	1	2	2	4	3	4	2		23
Annual Cases	10	12	15	12		14	21	21	21	41	44	55	46	61	67	77	517

Appendix C
Central Maine General Hospital Patient Statistics[1]

Table 1. Central Maine General Hospital Patients Survival Rates, 1893-1910

Year	Deceased Patients	Live Patients	Total Patients	Percent Lividity
1893	10	218	228	95.6%
1894	13	349	357	97.8%
1895	15	277	292	94.9%
1896	13	326	339	96.2%
1897	16	286	302	94.7%
1898	16	404	420	96.2%
1899	24	463	487	95.1%
1900	28	535	563	95.0%
1901	29	722	751	96.1%
1902	34	866	900	96.2%
1903	41	839	880	95.3%
1904	39	811	850	95.4%
1905	47	907	954	95.1%
1906	51	1010	1061	95.2%
1907	52	1023	1075	95.2%
1908	46	1058	1104	95.8%
1909	55	1143	1197	95.5%
1910	68	1162	1230	94.5%
Total	597	12399	12990	95.5%

Table 2. Central Maine General Hospital Patient Subsidization, 1893-1906[2]

Year	Free Treatment	Partial Subsidy	Total Subsidized	Paying Patients	Total Patients
1893	45	19	64	164	228
1894	132	28	160	202	362
1895	131	27	158	134	292
1896	148	21	169	170	339
1897	124	27	151	151	302
1898	224	44	268	152	420
1899	235	51	166	201	367
1900	248	40	288	275	563
1901	305	77	382	369	751
1902	381	67	448	452	900
1903	300	94	394	486	880
1904			119	731	850
1905			105	849	954
1906			122	939	1061
Total	2619	495	2994	5275	8269

Table 3. Central Maine General Hospital Patients Occupations, 1906-1909[3]

Year	Skilled Labor	Professionals	Unskilled Labor	Others
1906	7.9%	9.2%	28.7%	54.2%
1907	9.5%	7.8%	24.5%	58.2%
1908	8.6%	9.1%	27.6%	54.7%
1909	9.1%	9.2%	24%	57.3%

Table 4. Central Maine General Hospital Common Medical Conditions, 1893–1908[4]

Condition	Year																Total Cases
	1893	1894	1895	1896	1897	1898	1899	1900	1901	1902	1903	1904	1905	1906	1907	1908	
Abortion												3	4	3	7	2	19
Albuminaria				3	5												8
Addiction – Alcohol	1				1	2	2	2	4	3	3	3	6	5	6	7	48
Addiction – Morphine													1	1	2	2	6
Addiction – Opium	1			2	2					2	2						9
Anemia	1	3	2					2		4	12		1	1	4	1	31
Apoplexy	1	2		4	2	1	1	2		1	3	5	4	2		1	29
Asthma	1	1				1									1		4
Bronchitis	5	7	2	3	5	8	2	4	4		1	5	4	1	2	1	54
Cancer (all)	1		1		1		3			4	2				2		14
Cirrhosis of Liver										1	1	1		1	1	1	6
Cystitis	2	2	3	1	6	3	2	1		2	5					2	29
Delirium Tremens															1		1
Dementia											2				1		3
Diarrhea			1	1	1					1							4
Dysentery						1		1			1	1				1	4
Dyspepsia	1			2	3	1	1	5	6	10	10	7		5	4	4	59
Endometritus				8	5	1	1	1	3	6	1						26
Epilepsy	3	3	1			1	3	2	1	2		1	1	1			19

(continued)

Table 4. Central Maine General Hospital Common Medical Conditions, 1893–1908[4]

Condition	1893	1894	1895	1896	1897	1898	1899	1900	1901	1902	1903	1904	1905	1906	1907	1908	Total Cases
Exhaustion or /Debility													4		1	5	10
Gastro-related	9	6	11			8	6	5	9	5	8	3	8	2	2	8	90
Hepatitis		1	1		1	2	3	3	5	3	6						25
Heart Disease (all)	1	4	5		2	5	2	8	7	10	7		1	6	6	7	71
Hypochondria									2	1		1					4
Hysteria		5															5
Influenza		4	1					2	9	4	1	14	13	8	10	7	73
Insanity													3		2		5
Melancholia	1			1							1						3
Mania												1		3	2		6
Measles																4	4
Menstrual Complications	1	2	2		1			1	2					1			10
Miscarriage		1		2							4					3	10
Nervous Prostration														7			7
Neuralgia		2			4	1	4		2	1		3	1	1	1		22
Neurasthenia	2	3	8	6	3	6	5		12	15	17	13	11	1	10	11	123

(continued)

Table 4. Central Maine General Hospital Common Medical Conditions, 1893–1908[4] (continued)

Condition	Year																Total Cases
	1893	1894	1895	1896	1897	1898	1899	1900	1901	1902	1903	1904	1905	1906	1907	1908	
Obstetrics			1	2		1	5	9	12	9	15	10	25	30	38	35	192
Ovaritis	1																1
Pneumonia	6	5	2	4	3		9	1	2	5	6	4	14	17	6	16	100
Rheumatism (all)	2	9	4	4	7	3	3	7	10	10	9	11	12	8	11	12	122
Scrofula	1	3				1											5
Starvation													1	1			2
Syphilis or Gonorrhea	1	2	3			3	6	4	4	6	4	5	1	4		1	44
Tuberculosis							1	1	11	7	2	4	7	2	1	3	39
Typhoid Fever	10	16	4	8	6	11	10	8	27	18	13	14	22	27	4	7	205
Annual Cases	65	111	83	91	70	92	93	90	150	218	191	169	230	194	179	213	2239

Table 5. Central Maine General Hospital Causes of Death, 1893-1908[5]

Condition	1893	1894	1895	1896	1897	1898	1899	1900	1901	1902	1903	1904	1905	1906	1907	1908	Total Cases
Abscess/Infection					1	1	1			1	3	1	2	3		2	15
Alcoholism			1							1				2	1	5	10
Anemia		1															1
Appendicitis						1	1	3	4	1	8	9	6	7	4	3	47
Arterial Disease	1	1		2		1				2	2	1		4	1	1	16
Blood Disorders					1	1	1	1	1			1	1			2	9
Burns							1						1			2	4
Cancer	2	1	2	2	1	1	4	2	1	5	3	2	3	7	9	8	52
Gangrene				1	1	1		1		2				10			16
Gastro-Intestinal				1	1		1	1	1		5	1	1	4	3	5	24
Gynecological	2	3		2	1	5	8	8	10	9	3	6	5	2	9	3	76
Heart Disease		1	3	2	1	1		4	2	1	2			1		3	21
Hernia				1				1							3		5
Kidney Disorders	1	2		1	1					2	3	4	5	1	1	2	23
Meningitis	1			1				1	1	2			2			3	11

(continued)

Table 5. Central Maine General Hospital Causes of Death, 1893-1908[5] (continued)

Condition	Year																Total Cases
	1893	1894	1895	1896	1897	1898	1899	1900	1901	1902	1903	1904	1905	1906	1907	1908	
Pneumonia	2	2	1		1		3			3			4	3	4	6	29
Syphilis							1				1		1		1	1	5
Starvation												1	1		1		3
Trauma		2	6		5	2	1	4	2	2	3	5	2	2	2	3	41
Tuberculosis			1								1	1			2	2	6
Typhoid Fever			1		2		1	3	4		1		1		3		16
Other	1	1				1	2		3	3	3	3	11	4	3	1	37
Annual Deaths	10	14	15	13	16	14	25	29	29	34	38	35	46	50	47	52	467

Appendix D
Lewiston's Grey Nuns

This appendix is compiled from a collection of journals, record books, and the community's chronique located at the Grey Nuns' archive in Saint-Hyacinthe, Quebec.[1]

Information on each sister was never recorded in a consistent manner or always preserved. The movement of individual sisters as they traveled from one Grey Nun community or foundation furthermore acerbated the difficulty of tracking sisters and the detailing the work they accomplished. For example, there are two entries for Alphonsine Phaneuf at Hospital General Sainte-Marie. Yet they were two different sisters, who both worked in the Lewiston community but at different times. The majority of surviving records only list one name although they were two distinctively different women. When this occurred one of the sisters often selected a religious name by which they were known.

The use of an asterisk following a sister's name is to denote her status within the congregation as a petit sister. It was not uncommon for congregations of women religious to have two classes of sisters. The classes were distinguished by their education, prayer life and the form of physical labor they performed in the community. The petit sisters in the Grey Nuns worked and prayed as equals along side the fully professed Grey Nuns. They could not, however, be placed as a head of a department or elected the superior of the order. There was a slight variation in their habit. Both the veil and the cross that the petit sister wore were different from a professed Grey Nun. The petit sisters were fully integrated within the congregation in 1937.[2]

Records on sisters have also been lost as various institutions closed during the twentieth century or were simply never maintained. The privacy rules maintained by the Grey Nuns coupled with Canadian legal restrictions that prevent personal identification also have greatly restricted research and the publication of material.[3] The following list represents the most comprehensive study ever compiled on the Grey Nuns who were assigned to the Lewiston community and their institutions from 1878 to 1908.

The listing of each Grey Nun is not done alphabetically or chronologically, but rather, by the number they received upon their entrance into the Grey Nun congregation. Each woman is given a number when she joins the Grey Nuns, which reflects her numerical status as a sister within the community since its founding in 1840. No religious names are provided by request of the Grey Nuns.

NAME	BIRTH	DEATH	YEARS IN LEWISTON	OCCUPATION
Domithilde Phaneuf	4/6/1833	2/8/1911	1892	N/A
Alphonsine Cote	7/27/1830	10/25/1911	1878–1887	First Superior in Lewiston Community.
Adeline Bernard	1/10/1840	12/22/1918	1891–1893	Second Superior at the Asylum.
Helen Hogue	9/27/1843	1/2/1901	1886–1888	Superior, during expansion into the Golder Estate and the founding of the Asylum.
Ida Turgeon	8/15/1840	1/7/1916	1893	Nurse
Elizabeth Bouchard	1/21/1841	5/22/1945	N/A	N/A
Cedulie Desnoyers	7/22/1843	11/27/1888	1880	N/A
Thererise Vincelette	9/9/1842	9/29/1919	1905	N/A
Cesarie Brault	1/20/1848	12/14/1891	1880	Taught in the Asylum.
Emma Amoit	5/28/1846	5/4/1913	1896–5/1913	Worked in the dispensary.
Eugenie Archambault	7/25/1847	4/2/1930	3/1879–4/1880 1900–1902	Internship/ training. Sixth Superior at the Asylum.
Octavie Cardin	9/8/1851	2/1/1912	1892	N/A
Adeline Leblanc	7/15/1844	2/21/1917	1878–1880 1893–1897	Kitchen. Third Superior at the Asylum.

(continued)

NAME	BIRTH	DEATH	YEARS IN LEWISTON	OCCUPATION
Rosalie Galipeau	7/9/1847	10/20/1933	1878	Administration
Malvina Bourbonniere	7/17/1858	2/27/1951	12/1887–9/1889	One of the first sisters to work at the Asylum.
Sophie Brault	3/29/1852	11/1/1903	1891	N/A
Amanda Ferron	11/20/1849	1/10/1940	1889	N/A
Edesse Beauregard	4/11/1857	6/13/1919	1902	N/A
Corinne Frederic	4/19/1857	6/20/1933	12/1878 8/1903–4/1913	N/A N/A
Philomène Champoux	7/15/1847	8/27/1893	12/1878 1888	One of the first sisters to work at the Asylum.
Cordelie Dorval	8/19/1846	1/26/1929	12/31/1878 1897–1898	N/A. Fourth Superior at the Asylum.
Julie Dion	4/3/1851	12/29/1937	N/A	N/A
Dorila Peltier	4/2/1855	12/26/1940	4/1898–1900 1905–1910	Fifth Superior at the Asylum. In the Men's Ward.
Edwige Peloquin	8/25/1861	5/30/1937	1901	N/A
Emilie Bengle	9/1/1855	12/17/1899	1890	N/A
Dina Hevey	2/27/1856	5/24/1940	1903, 1913 1919–1930	N/A N/A
Justine Perras	11/8/1857	1/4/1930	1888–1891	First Superior at the Asylum.
Maria Casavant	8/23/1882	6/25/1894	1/1890–12/1893	N/A
Emma Belanger	11/16/1863	6/21/1896	1893	N/A
Malvina Dumaine	4/7/1863	5/27/1957	1890	N/A
Corine Phaneuf	8/19/1864	3/25/1943	1890-1916	N/A

(continued)

NAME	BIRTH	DEATH	YEARS IN LEWISTON	OCCUPATION
Alphonsine Phaneuf	3/5/1860	4/26/1903	1880	Convent. One of the first sisters to work at the Asylum.
Honorine Brodeur	1/18/1864	12/5/1938	1888 1892 1902–1907	Pharmacist/ Teacher. Surgical/General nursing. First Superior GHSM
Zéphyrine Duhamel	6/14/1853	3/24/1911	N/A	N/A
Georgienne Morin	1/9/1862	10/2/1948	N/A	N/A
Zoë Langlois	3/18/1862	10/7/1912	1891 8/1906–1912	N/A N/A
Theonile Chagnon	2/1/1859	8/21/1907	1906	N/A
Celina Dufresne	10/27/1862	7/29/1894	3/1890–9/1892	N/A
Rose-Anna Barbeau	2/23/1867	12/19/1954	1896 1907–1912	Orphanage. Second Superior at GHSM.
Rosalie Surette	2/29/1864	10/25/1893	N/A	N/A
Azilda Gingras	3/11/1891	9/6/1945	1893	N/A
Maria Caron	7/26/1870	9/7/1902	1896	N/A
Rose-Anna Fugere	3/31/1871	8/29/1959	1899	Kitchen, linen room
Anna l'Hérault*	8/26/1874	6/21/1956	N/A	N/A
Amelia Jodoin	6/30/1871	11/22/1952	1899	Kitchen
Ema Moison	10/4/1870	1/24/1907	1899	Pharmacist
Victorine Guertin	6/6/1872	2/21/1959	1894–1896	Gardener for orphans
Anna Beauregard	1/6/1874	7/20/1897	1896	Orphans
Eugenie Desautels	10/10/1868	3/5/1901	1897	Left Community
Albina Archambault[4]	1/3/1872	2/21/1961	1895 1897 1898 1908	Taught Orphans Nursed ill orphans Nursed women Lay nursing school
Delima Lalime	5/9/1868	8/16/1954	1904, 1929–30	N/A
Amanda Vallée*	10/19/1874	12/6/1969	1905–08	Infirmary
Georgienne Jacques[5]	12/25/1873	2/21/1902	1897–1901	N/A

(continued)

NAME	BIRTH	DEATH	YEARS IN LEWISTON	OCCUPATION
Jeannotte Alphonsine	4/26/1873	3/25/1948	1897, 1904	N/A
Elenore Paquette[6]	1/20/1873	1/20/1953	9–12/1902	Pharmacist, O.R.
Clara Morin	8/4/1864	3/6/1905	1903-06	Purchasing agent
Emma Beauregard	1/1/1873	3/7/1928	1897	N/A
Cordelia Masse	2/2/1864	4/28/1934	1898	N/A
Alphonsine Drapeau[7]	2/5/1871	6/13/1958	1908–13	Male geriatrics
Lumina Phaneuf	2/11/1873	8/15/1955	1900	N/A
Xaverine Brien	11/1/1870	3/29/1942	1901	N/A
Antonineth Maynard	12/6/1875	4/23/1910	N/A	N/A
Arzelie Guertin[8]	12/14/1874	4/11/1959	1904	Operating Room
Clara Brault	12/17/1873	11/17/1962	N/A	N/A
Aurelie Biron*[9]	7/29/1877	11/4/1960	1899 1900	Kitchen Medical supplies
Olivine Duguay	7/7/1878	12/31/1962	1905–23	Kitchen
Marie-Anna Millette[10]	7/12/1875	1/8/1971	1906	Orphans

Notes

NOTES TO THE LIST OF FIGURES

1. Figures 1, 10, 12, 14, 23, 25, 26 are copyright The Sisters of Charity, Saint-Hyacinthe and The Sisters of Charity, Montreal and appear with their permission. Figures 4–9, 15–22 are copyright 2005 by Susan P. Hudson, Ph.D. and may not be used without the author's consent. Figures 2, 3, 11, 13, and 24 are in the public domain.

NOTES TO THE PREFACE

1. There are several studies written on the founding history of the Grey Nuns and Marguerite d'Youville's dynamic spirituality. While the majority of these works are historically accurate the language used in the texts is often an euphemistic style that belittled the magnitude of both Marguerite d'Youville and her order's accomplishments. See Rev. P. Duchaussois, *The Grey Nuns in the Far North* (Toronto: McClelland and Stewart, Ltd.1919); Mary Paul Fitts, *Hands to the Needy, Marguerite d'Youville Apostle to the Poor Foundress of the Grey Nuns* (Garden City: Doubleday and Company, 1987); Estelle Mitchell, *Father Charles Dufrost and His Mother 1729–1790*, trans. Antoinette Bezaire (Montreal: Meridian Press, 1990); *Marguerite d'Youville, Foundress of the Grey Nuns,* trans. Helena Nantaiz, (Montreal, 1949); Estelle Mitchell, *The Spiritual Portrait of Saint Marguerite d'Youville,* trans. Joanna Kerwin and Antoinette Bezaire (Quebec: The Grey Nuns of Montreal, 1993); Antoine Sattin, *Life of Mother d'Youville, Foundress and First Superior of the Sister of Charity or Grey Nuns,* trans. Georgiana Michaud (Montreal: Meridien, 1999). The most comprehensive and current work on Marguerite d'Youville is Albertine Ferland-Angers, *Mother d'Youville, First Canadian Foundress,* trans. Richard R. Cooper (Montreal: The Sisters of Charity, Montreal, 2000), esp. 66–70. Scholarship pertaining to particular Grey Nun communities is slim. There are two solid works on the Saint-Hyacinthe community which references to other Grey Nun community's both are located at the Sisters

of Charity of Saint-Hyacinthe Archives (hereafter cited as SOCSHA). The two works are *En Feuilletant les Chroniques, de l'Hôtel-Dieu de Saint-Hyacinthe et des Maisons qui en Dependent documents Maskoutains No. 12 1840–1940,* (Saint-Hyacinthe: Société D'Histoire Religionale, 1940); and Gagnon, *La Maison Jaune.*

2. Rachel Naomi Remen, M.D. *Kitchen Table Wisdom, Stories that Heal,* 38.
3. Unpublished notes of Sister Marie-Paule Messier, Archivist, SOCSHA.
4. Maher, *To Bind Up the Wounds,* 99.
5. *Constitutions Et Règles, De La Congregation des Soeurs de la Charité de Saint-Hyacinthe,* Chapter General 1982, 45, trans. Sister Jacqueline Peloquin, and Susan Hudson, SOCSHA.
6. For a more nuanced discussion of this point see James Hillman, *We've had a Hundred Years of Psychotherapy and the World is Getting Worse,* 140.
7. Nancy Cott, *The Bonds of Womanhood: "Woman's Sphere" in New England, 1780–1835,* 140.
8. The French term "pensionnaires" connotes a woman who usually paid to live with the sisters within their foundations or convent. She may have done light work for the community or been ill and required care. Or she could have been a widow in need of community. The arrangement varied with each situation. *Constitutions Et Règles, De la Congregation des Soeurs de la Charité de Saint-Hyacinthe,* trans. Sister Jacqueline Peloquin and Susan Hudson, SOCSHA.
9. Motto cited in *Marguerite d'Youville, Great Moments in Canadian Church History* (Canada), 16. Notes from interview with Sister Jacqueline Peloquin, April 16, 2001 also substantiated this finding.
10. Quoted in Peter Gossage, *Families in Transition, Industry and Population in Nineteenth-Century Saint-Hyacinthe,* 48, trans. Peloquin and Hudson.
11. *Ibid.*
12. *En Feuilletant les Chroniques de l'Hôtel-Dieu de S.-Hyacinthe, Et Des Maison En Dependent, 1840–1940 Documents Maskoutains No. 12,* 120–121. SOCSHA.
13. *Ibid.* 18.
14. Interview, Sister Jacqueline Peloquin, October 30, 2001.

NOTES TO THE INTRODUCTION

1. Kauffman, *Ministry & Meaning,* 25.
2. Nelson, *Say Little,* 54; Patricia Wittenberg, "Back to the Future: The Current Paradigm Shift in Women's Religious Communities," paper read at the History of Women Religious Conference, Milwaukee, Wisconsin (June 19, 2001), 2. This argument is also supported in Kenneally, *The History of American Catholic Women,* esp. 43–59; and Margaret Susan Thompson,

"To Serve the People of God: Nineteenth-Century Sisters and the Creation of an American Religious Life," *Working Paper Series* 18, 2 (Spring 1987).
3. Patricia Wittberg, "Back to the Future," 3.
4. See Appendix D.
5. *Ibid*, 2.
6. *Ibid;* SOCSHA; Copies of private papers in author's possession.
7. Farren, *A Call to Care*, 94.

NOTES TO CHAPTER ONE

1. All statistics are from the *Tenth Annual Report of the Sisters' Hospital of Lewiston, Maine, Souvenir Number Nineteen Hundred & Two*, 3, 24–25, SOCSHA.
2. *Sisters' Hospital Tenth Annual Report:* 1902, 26, SOCSHA. Gagnon, *La Maison Jaune*, 267–277, SOCSHA. These statistics on the number of Grey Nun novices and professed sisters does not include women who left the order prior to their final profession.
3. Chronique, "Soeur Honorine Brodeur: dite Marie-de-l'Incarnation," SOCSHA.
4. *Ibid.*
5. *Ibid.*
6. *Sixteenth Annual Report Hospital of the Sisters of Charity, Lewiston, Maine*, 18, SOCSHA.
7. *Ibid.*
8. *Ibid*, 19.
9. *Ibid.*
10. Saint Mary's nursing school was closed in June 1988. The building was demolished September 2001. Documents pertaining to the institution are located at SOCSHA and SOCHA.
11. Cabinet no. 25, File, "Religious Women," letter dated June 19, 1903. This single letter represents the entire collection, PCA.
12. *Ibid.*
13. Darrel W. Amundsen, provides an insightful argument on the interconnection of medicine and faith in early Christianity; one that continues to prevail in some contemporary theologies. See Darrel W. Amundsen, "Medicine and Faith in Early Christianity," Bulletin of the History of Medicine 56 (1982): 343.

NOTES TO CHAPTER TWO

1. Binder, "Clergy D-K," PCA.
2. Chronique, No. 69, trans. Peloquin and Hudson, SOCSHA.
3. *Ibid.*
4. Files. Mission Effectiveness Office. SOCHA.
5. *Ibid.* For information on the individual woman that joined the Sisters of Sion in Maine, and where their vocation as a Sion led them following the order's departure from Maine contact author for private papers.

6. The scholarship on this topic is broad. See Linda Gordon ed. *Women, the State, and Welfare,* esp. 9–123; Irving Howe, *World of our Fathers;* Janet Wilson James, "Women in American Religion," ed. Janet William James *Women in American Religion,* 1–15; Nelson. *Say Little.*

7. Thomas Lee Philpott, *The Slum and the Ghetto: Immigrants, Blacks, and Reformers in Chicago, 1880–1930,* 82. For a brief discussion on specifically French-Canadian welfare structures see Mark Paul Richards, "Coping before l'Etat-providence: Collective Welfare Strategies of New England's Franco-Americans:" 59–67.

8. Herve-B. LeMaire's use of the term Franco-American in his otherwise admirable study on the survival of the French language in New England is incorrect. A Franco-American designates a child born of French Canadian parents in the United States. This distinction that Yves Frenette takes drastic measures to ensure so that the non French Canadian population does not misuse the term. LeMaire argues that it was the Franco-Americans who were responsible for the maintenance of the French language in New England not French Canadians. In Lewiston it was a more complex process as bilingualism was not an intergenerational issue into the mid-twentieth century. This consequently involved several generations and continual immigration from Quebec, not just first-born Franco-Americans in Maine. See Herve-B. LeMaire, "Franco-American Efforts on Behalf of the French Language in New England" Joshua A. Fishman et al., *Language Loyalty in the United States,* 253.

9. C.J. Nuesse and Thomas J. Harte, *The Sociology of the Parish,* 156.

10. Philip Gleason, *Keeping the Faith, American Catholicism Past and Present,* 42.

11. As quoted in Robert Rumilly, *Histoire des Franco-Américains,* 204. James E. Cassidy would have a long and distinguish career in the Catholic church. He was appointed Titular Bishop of Ibora and Auxiliary to the diocese of Fall River in 1930. He would succeed to the Fall River See on July 28, 1934 and remain until his death on May 17, 1951. See, *Official Catholic Directory Anno Domini 1998,* 381. The thrust to Americanize the immigrants was led by Cardinal James Gibbons of Baltimore (1834–1921), Archbishop John Ireland of St. Paul (1838–1918), and Archbishop John Keane, first rector of the Catholic University of America and Archbishop of Dubuque, (1839–1918), and Bishop Denis O'Connell of Richmond and of the North American College in Rome. For a deeper discussion of the Americanist controversy see Philip Gleason, *Keeping the Faith,* 41–43.

12. Dorothy M. Brown and Elizabeth McKeown, *The Poor Belong to Us, Catholic Charities and American Welfare.*

13. Chronique No. 79.

14. *Ibid.*

15. Visites de La Supérieure Générale, 1883–1909. SOCSHA.

16. Chronique No. 79

17. *Ibid.*

NOTES TO CHAPTER THREE

1. A. M. Myhrman and J.A. Rademaker, "The Second Colonization Process in an Industrial Community," 11.
2. *Ibid.*
3. Myhrman and Rademaker, "The Second Colonization," 12.
4. *Ibid.* For information on the parish of Saint Louis, See files located at PCA.
5. *Ibid.* 4.
6. There is a lack of consensus on the precise dates for the various Mills due to confusion over the time when full operation was achieved and the date of establishment, or if the name of the mill changed ownership. Furthermore as the Mills declined and were eventually abandoned archival material was lost or destroyed. These dates and the information on the mills and bleacherys were collected from the following sources; see Reverend Frank Morin, "A parish Was Needed," *Lewiston Sun Journal* (Saturday April 10, 1982), 2A; Binder, Parish Histories, "Saint Joseph," "Saints Peter and Paul," PCA: *Paroisse Canadienne-Francaise de Lewiston (Maine) album Hisotrique Public par Les Petes Dominicans, 1899,* 21–22, SPPA; Myhrman and Rademaker, "the Second colonization," 4–5.
7. *Ibid.*
8. *Ibid.*
9. Ralph Vicero, "Sources statistiques pour l'étude de l'immigration et du peuplement Canadien-Francais en Nouvelle-Angleterre au cours XIXe siècle," *Initiating Franco-American Studies* Stanley L. Freeman, Jr. and Raymond J. Pelletier. While Vicero's work is prodigious on the geographical movement of French Canadians into the United States it must be viewed with caution as record keeping was not systematic.
10. Myhrman and Rademaker, "The Second Colonization," 17.
11. Validation Book, 1883, City Clerk Vault, City of Lewiston.
12. Papers, SOCHA.
13. Yves Frenette, "Understanding the French Canadians," 207–208; Lucey, *The Catholic Church,* 167.
14. Dingley, *Historical Sketch of Lewiston,* 10, 21–23, Quoted in Yves Frenette, "Understanding the French Canadians of Lewiston," 201.
15. Myhrman and Rademaker, "The Second Colonization," 15. Nelson Dingley, Jr. *Historical Sketch of Lewiston* (Lewiston Journal, 1871), 10, 21–23. Quoted in Yves Frenette, "Understanding the French Canadians of Lewiston," 20l.
16. Binder, Parish Histories "Lewiston, 1853–1955," 1. PCA.
17. Madeleine Giguere, *To Make a Living: Franco American Work Traditions in Lewiston and Auburn.*
18. Parker, "History of the Franklin Company and Related Enterprise," LPL, 4.
19. For studies pertaining to these and other ethnic communities in urban America, I recommend the following works; Gary Gerstle, *Working Class Americanism: The Politics of Labor in a Textile City, 1914–1960;* Tamara

K. Hareven, *Family time and Industrial time;* Hareven, ed., *Family and Kin in Urban Communities,* esp. 189–202; for specific information on another French Canadian immigrant community, see Tamara K. Hareven and Randolph Langenbach, *Amoskeag, Life and Work in the American Factory-City.*

20. Frances H. Early wrote an insightful article on the cultural value that a Little Canada held to the immigrating French Canadian family in "The Settling-In Process: The Beginnings of the Little Canada in Lowell, Massachusetts, in the Late Nineteenth Century," *Steeples and Smokestacks* ed. Clare Quintal, 89–108; esp. 104. A more colorful historical account of French Canadian immigration and the formation of a little Canada can be found in Iris Saunders Podea, "Quebec to "Little Canada:" The Coming of the French Canadians to New England in the Nineteenth Century," ed. Madeleine Giguere, *A Franco-American Overview, Vol. 3 New England,* 113–123.

21. Jay P. Dolan. *Catholic Revivalism: The American Experience 1830–1900,* 10–25–26.

22. *New Catholic Encyclopedia,* Vol. VI (McGraw-Hill Books, 1967), 143; Wade expands his argument and provides supporting evidence in his article "French and French Canadians in the U.S." ed. Madeleine Giguere A *Franco-American Overview,* 37–45.

23. Ralph Dominic Vicero, "Immigration of French Canadians to New England, 1840–1900: A Geographical Analysis" Ph.D. dissertation, University of Wisconsin, 1968, 275.

24. Yves Roby, *Les Franco-Americans De La Nouvelle-Angleterre 1776–1930.* Note that records from Saint Pierre indicate a different number for these years: 5,233 attending Saint Pierre in 1800 and 12,546 in 1900.

25. See Appendix A.

NOTES TO CHAPTER FOUR

1. Binder, History of Parishes, "Saint Joseph," PCA.
2. Lucey, *The Catholic Church,* 166.
3. Myhrman and Rademaker, "The Second Colonization," 15.
4. Binder II, "History of Parishes," PCA.
5. Myhrman and Rademaker, "The Second Colonization," 15.
6. The article was printed in the *Lewiston Evening Journal,* "Builder of Lewiston, Death of Capt. Albert H. Kelsey in Cambridge Aged 90 years. Man who Built the Mills, Streets, Parks and Hotel in This City: An Interview with Him Republished from the Journal a Year Ago," (March 4, 1901), Microfiche Collection, LPL; Kelsey is referring to the American Protective Association. The APA was an anti-Catholic and anti-immigrant secret society founded by Henry F. Bower at Clinton, Iowa in 1887. What is of interest here is that the burning of Saint John's chapel predates the founding of this society by nineteen years. Yet Kelsey refers to it. Obviously the bigotry which supported the

founding of the APA was paralleled in Lewiston's Protestant community, almost two decades prior to being formally institutionalized. See Glazier and Shelley, eds. *The Encyclopedia of American Catholic History,* 93–95.

7. *Lewiston Evening Journal,* "Builder of Lewiston, Death of Capt. Albert H. Kelsey," 2, LPL; Henry Gosselin, "St. Patrick's in Lewiston, Celebrates 100 years of ethnic harmony on May 3," *The Church World,* (April 26, 1990), 18–20; Binder History of Parishes, "Saint Joseph," PCA; File "Parish History, Saint Joseph's Parish The First 125 years," Rectory Vault, Saint Joseph Parish, Lewiston, Maine. All quotations are reproduced as they were used in the text.

8. File "Parish History, Saint Joseph's Parish The First 125 years," Rectory Vault, Saint Joseph Parish, Lewiston, Maine.

9. Binder, Parish Histories "Saint Joseph," PCA. File "Parish History, Saint Joseph's Parish The First 125 years," Rectory Vault, Saint Joseph Parish, Lewiston, Maine.

10. Parish Reports Box, 1879, copy of chancery letter-files, "Lewiston Agreement, Saints Patrick's and Joseph's, -March 1895," PCA.

11. See *First Annual Report on Birth, Marriages, Divorces and Deaths, in the State of Maine, Year ending December 31, 1892* (Augusta: Burleigh & Flynt, 1894).

12. For tables that illustrate the break down of the approximate numbers of French Canadians immigrants to the United States and New England per decade from 1860–1900. See, Yves Roby, *Les Franco-Américain,* 34, tables 2, 3.

13. Drawer, "Lewiston, Saints Peter and Paul," File, "Saints Peter and Paul," PCA.

14. Yves Roby, *Les Franco-Américains de la Nouvelle-Angleterre 1776–1930* (Quebec: Septentrion, 1990), esp. 63, 68; James W. Serles, dir. *Immigrants for the North,* (Bath: 1982), 50; Madeleine Giguere, *To Make a Living,* B5; Myhrman and Rademaker, "The Second Colonization," 18. An extensive historical demographic analysis of French Canadian immigration is constructed in Ralph Dominic Vicero's dissertation "Immigration of French Canadians to New England," There is a rather suspect claim made by the local Lewiston newspaper that French Canadians were arriving in Lewiston at the rate of 100 to 150 per day by the 1875. See, *Sun Journal,* Lewiston, Maine (Sunday, July 14, 2002), B5.

15. Madeleine Giguere, *To Make A Living,* 2.

16. Josaphat Benoit, *L'ame Franco-Américaine,* 51; Madeleine Giguere, *To Make a Living,* 4, Myhrman and Rademaker, "The Second Colonization," 20.

17. Laura Offenhartz Greene, *Child Labor Then and Now,* 64, 270–275.

18. The ethnicities listed in the 1880 census were: United States, Ireland, Germany, Great Britain, Sweden, Norway, British American, Other Countries. See, *Tenth Census of the United States, Volume I 1880,* Population, tables of Occupation 703–909, Maine State Library (hereafter cited as MSL); *Eleventh Census of the United States 1890,* Population, II, 564–565 MSL; The importance of the *Eleventh Census* as a primary source for indicating

the employment patterns of French Canadians in Maine was also acknowledged by James Paul Allen, *Catholics in Maine*, Table 5, 153.

19. Myhrman and Rademaker, "The Second Colonization," 29.
20. Ethnic segregation among Catholic immigrant communities who lived within the same metropolitan area was not unusual. See, Robert Anthony Orsi, *The Madonna of 115ᵗʰ Street, Faith and Community in Italian Harlem, 1880–1950.*
21. Mason Wade, "French and French Canadians in the U.S." ed. Madeleine Giguere *A Franco-American Overview*, 41.
22. The statistic that places the founding of Saint Pierre parish as the eleventh national French Canadian parish in New England is drawn from the research of William MacDonald. There is an error however in MacDonald's work. He recorded that the founding of Saint Pierre was in 1869 not 1870. See William MacDonald, "The French Canadians in New England," ed. Madeleine Giguere *A Franco-American Overview*, 1–22, esp. 3.
23. Binder History of Parishes, "Catholic Beginnings in Lewiston," 1, PCA.
24. Marie P. Badeau, et al. *SS. Peter and Paul Parish*, 11.
25. Hevey file. SPPA.
26. As quoted in Madeleine Giguere and Carmel Laverdiere, *Chronology,* 1, SPPA.
27. Libby Mill Payroll Carding and Spinning Department 1908–1915. This collection is currently being archived by the Lewiston Public Library, Lewiston, Maine.
28. *Cinquantenaire de l'Institut Jacques-Cartier* (Lewiston, 1925), 5; quoted in Yves Frenette, *Understanding the French Canadians,* 209. For a fully discussion of similar French Canadian mutual aid societies see Yves Roby, *Les Franco-Américains, 126–129.*
29. Frenette, *Op. Cit,* 210.
30. See, Saint Peter and Paul Necrology, Saint Peter and Paul Cemetery, Switzerland Road, Lewiston, Maine. Only information on record.

NOTES TO CHAPTER FIVE

1. *Seventeenth Annual Report of the Receipts and Expenditures of the City of Lewiston for the Year Ending February 28, 1880, 11–12.*
2. Douglas Hodgkin, "Managing the Poor in Lewiston, Miane 1795–1863," Presented at Washburn Humanities Conference, Norlands, Livermore, Maine, June 2001. 2, 12–17.
3. Quote from the title of, Robert H. Wiebe, *The Search For Order 1877–1920.*
4. Hodgkin, *Op. Cit.,* 2.
5. Lewiston Town Record, I: 475, as quoted in Hodgkin, "Managing the Poor," 10–11.
6. Hodgkin, *Op. Cit.,* 10–12.
7. Vogel J. Morris, "The Transformation of the American Hospital, 1850–1920," *Health Care in America,* eds. Susan Reverby and David Rosner, 106.

8. An extensive collection of material on this facility is located in Box 65, FAHC.

9. *Report of the City Auditor Commencing with the first day of March 1863, and ending with the last day of February 29, 1864,* 61.

10. Charles E. Rosenberg, "Social Class and Medical Care in Nineteenth-Century America, The Rise and Fall of the Dispensary," *Journal of the History of Medicine* 29 (January 1974): 52.

11. The financial accounting of both the poor farm and alms house were yearly recorded in the *Annual Report of the Receipts and Expenditures of the City of Lewiston,* LPL.

12. Jay P. Dolan, *The Immigrant Church;* James Gilbert, *Perfect Cities, Chicago's Utopias of 1893,* esp. 1–22. Charles E. Rosenberg, "And Heal The Sick: The Hospital and the Patient in the 19th Century America," *Journal of Social History* 10 (Summer 1977): 428–447; Charles E. Rosenberg, "The Origins of the American Hospital System," *Bulletin of New York Academy of Medicine* 55 (January 1979): 10–21; Morris J. Vogel, *The Invention of the Modern Hospital, 1870–1930.*

13. Rosenberg, "The Origins of the American Hospital System," 14.

14. *Fifteenth Annual Report of the Receipts and Expenditures of the City of Lewiston for the fiscal year ending February 28, 1878,* 69.

15. *Thirty-fifth Annual Report of the Receipts and Expenditures of the City of Lewiston for the fiscal year ending February 28, 1898,* 141.

16. Charles E. Rosenburg, *The Care of Strangers: The Rise of America's Hospital System,* 15.

17. See, S.P. Hudson "Medicine for the Masses: The Social Dynamics of Lewiston Hospitals, 1888–1910," Washburn Humanities Conference, Norlands, Maine, June 1–3, 2000. Quotation from, *The Lewiston Journal, Illustrated Magazine,* September 28-October 3, 1901, Central Maine General Hospital File, Androscoggin County Historical Society, Auburn Maine (hereafter cited as ACHS).

18. J. M. Toner, Statistics of Regular Medical Associations and Hospitals in the United States, *Transactions of the American Medical Association* 24 (1872–1873): 320.

19. Report of the City Auditor Commencing with the First Day of March 1863, and Ending with the last day of February 1864, 31–32.

20. *Seventh Annual Report of the Receipts and Expenditures of the City of Lewiston for the fiscal year ending February 28, 1870,* 24–26, 40.

21. *Fifteenth Annual Report of the Receipts and Expenditures of the City of Lewiston for the fiscal year ending February 28, 1878,* 28, 45, 53.

22. *Thirtieth Annual Report of the Receipts and Expenditures of the City of Lewiston for the fiscal year ending February 28, 1893,* 15.

23. *Ibid.*

24. *Ibid,* 115.

25. The Triangle Shirtwaist Company fire of 1911 in New York City remains a tragic testament to the working conditions of many immigrant wage-laborers. 146 workers, mostly Jewish and Italian immigrant women, were

burned to death in a garment factory directly due to violations of fire code and management policy. See Irving Howe, *World of Our Fathers: The Journey of the East European Jews to America and the Life They Found and Made*, 298, 304–305.

26. *Thirty-Fifth Annual Report of the Receipts and Expenditures of the City of Lewiston, for the fiscal year ending February 28, 1898*, 16.

27. Philip T. Silvia, Jr. "Neighbors from the North; French-Canadian Immigrants vs. Trade Unionism in Fall River," ed. Claire Quintal. In *Steeple and Smokestacks*, 145, 161.

28. *Massachusetts, Bureau of Statistics of Labor, Thirteenth Annual Report, 1882*, 90.

29. See for example, Pay Roll May 1, 1909-January 23, 1915, Libby Mill Archival Collection, Lewiston Public Library.

NOTES TO CHAPTER SIX

1. Sommaire, September 1885- September 1888, 3–7, SOCHA.

2. For a detailed account of the establishment of a hospital by the Androscoggin County Medical Association (hereafter cited as ACMA), see "Establishing A Need," Public Relations Office, Central Maine Medical Center, Lewiston, Maine. This account, however, lacks any historical annotation to verify the material.

3. *First Annual Report: Central Maine General Hospital, Lewiston, Miane July 1, 1891-July 2, 1892*, 8. CMMC.

4. Drawer, "Lewiston Parishes," File, "Saint Peter and Paul," Box Parish Records, File "Lewiston, Saint Peter and Paul" Drawer, "Bishop Healy," File, "correspondence," PCA

5. *Ibid.*

6. "Engagement de L'Asile N.D. de Lourdes avec Monseigneur Hevey au Su. Don de \$12,000, 23 Mars 1891," trans. Peloquin and Hudson, SOCSHA. A further insight into Hevey's rather strange perception of his own exploitive behavior of the Grey Nuns is that in the document he does not have the scribe record his name. Rather he is referred to as the "Reverend Donator."

7. Sister Mary Denis Maher, *To Bind Up the Wounds*, 21.

8. *Hospital of the Sisters of Charity. Lewiston, Maine, 1894*, 3, SOCSHA.

9. Journal, *1884–1894*, "1888." SOCHA.

10. Chronique, "June 20, 1888." SOCSHA.

11. Androscoggin County Registry of Deeds, Book 129, 266; ACCH. Sister St. Charles was born Helen Hogue in Sherbrooke, Quebec on September 27, 1843. She entered the religious life at Saint-Hyacinthe in 1860. Professed as a Grey Nun on August 26, 1862. She died at the age of fifty-eight on January 2, 1901. Gagnon, *La Maison Jaune*, 269. SOCSHA.

12. Gagnon, *La Maison Jaune*, 269. SOCSHA.

13. Annales de la Communauté 1888, trans. Peloquin, SOCSHA.

14. *Second Annual Report of the Hospital and Orphanage of the Sisters of Charity For 1894, Lewiston, Maine, 1895*. 3. SOCSHA.

15. *Ibid.*
16. *Seventh Annual Report of the Hospital of the Sisters of Charity, Lewiston, Maine*, 1899, 6. SOCSHA.
17. *Ibid.*
18. Chronique, "Novmber 29, 1888. SOCSHA.
19. *First Annual Report Central Maine General Hospital: Lewiston, Maine July 1, 1891–1892.* 8, CMMC.
20. Chronique, No. 2. SOCSHA.
21. Bishop's Healy's papers and diary, PCA.
22. Box 103, "Franco American Doctors," FAHC.
23. Quoted in Kenneally, *The History of American Catholic Women*, 84.
24. Annual Reports, SOCSHA.
25. *Second Annual Report of the Hospital and Orphanage of the Sisters of Charity for 1894. Lewiston, Maine, 1995,* 3. SOCSHA.
26. Annales, 1888. SOCSHA.
27. *First Annual Report Central Maine General Hospital: Lewiston, Maine. July 1, 1891–1892.* 7–8, CMMC.
28. *First Annual Report Central Maine General Hospital: Lewiston, Maine. July 1, 1891–1892.* 11; *Second Annual Report Central Maine General Hospital: Lewiston, Maine. July 1, 1892–1893.* 10, CMMC.
29. *Fifth Annual Report of the Directors of the Central Maine General Hospital, Lewiston Maine.* 7, CMMC.
30. *Ninth Annual Report Hospital of the Sisters of Charity: Lewiston, Maine 1902.* 7. SOCSHA.
31. Interview with Sister Jacqueline Peloquin, Superior Portland, April 16, 2001.
32. *Fourth Annual Report of the Hospital of the Sisters of Charity, November 30, 1896: Lewiston, Maine,* 5. SOCSHA.
33. *Ibid.* 6.
34. *Lewiston Journal, Illustrated Magazine* (September 28-October 3, 1901), 10, File, "Central Maine General Hospital," AHSA.
35. *Acte Incorporation des Soeurs de Lewiston 2 Juillet 1892.* SOCSHA; Androscoggin Country Registry of Deeds, State of Maine Certificate of Organization, Book 971, 51, ACCH.
36. Philpott, *The Slum and the Ghetto,* 82.
37. Hevey is charging a 6% interest rate from the Grey Nuns while Sarah Golder only required a 5% interest rate for the mortgage on her estate; see, Androscoggin County Registre of Deeds, Book, 129, 265. ACCH.
38. *Engagement de l'Asile N.D. de Lourdes avec Monsignor Hevey au su. du don de $12,000.00 23 Mars 1891,* trans. Peloquin and Hudson. SOCSHA.
39. C.T. Onions, ed. *The Oxford Universal Dictionary on Historical Principles* (Oxford: Oxford University Press, 1933), 551.
40. *Annual Report of the Girls' Orphanage of Lewiston, Maine Under the auspices of the Sisters of Charity,* 1908, 7, SOCSHA
41. Chroniques, SOCSHA; private notes by Sister Jacqueline Peloquin, Portland, Me.

42. The names of the physicians were: A. Garcelon, Donovan, Fuller, Gerrish, Sanger, Thayer, Martin, Hitchcock, Martel, A.M. Garcelon, Dixon, Matte, Hawkins, Girouard, Dumont, Letourneau, Laroche, and Lupien. *Second Annual Report of the Hospital and Orphanage of the Sisters of Charity for 1894.* Lewiston: 1895, 1, SOCSHA.

43. The Grey Nuns recorded the awarding of State funding to their hospital in the annals and mentioned that "the Senate [had] only one Catholic." They possibly perceived this event as an act of religious tolerance and acceptance by Maine politicians, Annales *1894*, SOCSHA.

44. Data drawn from CMGH annual reports; *Annual Report Central Maine General Hospital, Lewiston, Maine: 1893, CMMC; Annual Reports of the Hospital of the Sisters of Charity: 1889, 1890, 1891, 1892, 1893, 1894, 1902,* SOCSHA; Sommaire, 1885–1904. SOCHA.

45. *Sisters Hospital Tenth Annual Report, 1902.* 27, SOCSHA

46. *Fourteenth Annual Report Hospital of the Sisters of Charity, Lewiston, Maine,* 10, SOCSHA. This may also have been a gentle form of manipulation by the Grey Nuns. By publicizing which doctors were using their hospital they applied pressure on those who did not practice there.

47. *Lewiston Journal, Illustrated Magazine,* (February 2, 1901) File, "Central Maine General Hospital," AHSA.

48. *Annual Report of St. Mary's General Hospital, Founded in 1888, Incorporated in 1892, 1910,* 15, SOCSHA. The Grey Nuns did not maintain annual reports of their hospital prior to the years before its incorporation in 1892. This was verified by the Grey Nun archivist Sister Mary-Paule Messier, Correspondence with author, April 9, 2001.

49. Compiled from data contained in the *Annual Report of the Hospital of the Sisters of Charity, Lewiston, Maine, 1893–1898. SOCSHA.*

50. Compiled from data contained in the *Annual Report Central Maine General Hospital, Lewiston, Maine, 1893–1898.* CMMC.

51. *Hospital of the Sisters of Charity of Lewiston, Maine Annual Report. 1896–1898.* 17–19, SOCSHA.

52. *Hospital of the Sisters of Charity of Lewiston, Maine 1888–1903. Eleventh Annual Report,* 10, SOCSHA; Charlotte Michaud, "Franco-American" *Lewiston Sun Journal,* (April 17, 1976).

53. *Hospital of the Sisters of Charity of Lewiston, Maine 1888–1903, Eleventh Annual Report,* 10, SOCSHA.

54. *Seventh Annual Report of the Hospital of the Sisters of Charity, Lewiston, Maine, 1899,* 6, SOCSHA. This report is also available at the University of Maine, Lewiston Auburn Franco-American Collection, Box 67, Lewiston, ME. FAHC.

55. Chronique, 4, SOCSHA. The Lady Patronesses Hospital Society was organized in 1898.

56. *Ibid.* 15; Sommaire, 1885–1904, SOCHA. Minor inconsistencies exist on the total numbers of patient admissions. I prefer to use the information from the Sommaire, when available, over the information found in the annual reports. The data in the Sommaire contains a more detailed

accounting of patients and orphans. The annual reports do not separate patient counts as precisely as the Sommaire.

57. Chronique, "1899," SOCSHA.
58. *Ibid.* 7.
59. Chroniques, SOCSHA.
60. Annale, 4. SOCSHA.

NOTES TO CHAPTER SEVEN

1. *Fourth Annual Report of the Hospital of the Sisters of Charity: For the Year Ending November 30, 1896, Lewiston, Maine,* 9, SOCSHA.
2. Drawer "Bishop Healy," File "Healy Asylum, letter between Reverend Edward Hurley and Bishop James Healy, March 2, 1900," PCA.
3. See Appendix B.
4. Ann Doyle, "Nursing by Religious Orders in the United States," 966; Sister Mary Denis Maher, *To Bind Up the Wounds,* 28.
5. Registre 1 & 2, 1880–1906, Entries numbered 248, 249, 251, 252, SOCHA.
6. Both parents were recorded consecutively as #248 and #249. Patient 250 was the daughter of one Francois Bernier. The Carpentier children were then admitted as patients #251 and #252. See Note 4 above.
7. Registre 1 & 2, 1880–1906, #316–320, SOCHA.
8. *Ibid.*
9. Phone interview with parish secretary, Saint Mary's Catholic Church, Bath, Maine, April 17, 2001 and confirmed by material held at the Portland Chancery Archives, Drawer "Bath, Saint Mary's," File "Saint Mary," PCA. This parish was founded in 1849.
10. No occupation was listed for Jeanne Montez Carpentier. Registre 1 & 2, 1880–1906, #249, #476.
11. Registre 1 & 2, 1880–1906, #248, #320, #475, SOCHA.
12. Registre 1 & 2, 1880–1906, #475–478, SOCHA.
13. The author has found no other information related to the Carpentier family after the death of Jeanne Carpentier and the discharge of her children. One only hopes that they experienced a full share of joy in the future to balance their sorrow.

NOTES TO CHAPTER EIGHT

1. As previously mentioned, the term Franco-American, to denote a second generation French Canadian, is not applicable here.
2. Data taken from the *Annual Reports of the Sisters of Charity Hospital, Saint Mary's General Hospital, 1900–1908,* SOCSHA.
3. *Seventh Annual Report of the Hospital of the Sisters of Charity, Lewiston, Maine, 1899,* 6 & 16 SOCSHA.
4. *Annual Reports of the Hospital of the Sisters of Charity, Lewiston, Maine,* 1888–1910. SOCSHA.

5. Averages of occupation classes based on Table 3, Appendix B and Table 3, Appendix C.

6. This information was irregularly characterized and reported by both hospitals in their annual reports. For comparative purposes, four consecutive years for each hospital were selected for calculation of percentages of occupations; since this data was not reported for all years, this meant that different four year periods were selected for each hospital. The occupation categories were developed by the author in the following manner: skilled craftsmen (carpenters, masons, painters, printers, shoemakers, etc.) classed as Skilled Labor; office and formally educated workers (managers, clerks, doctors, nurses, ship captains, etc.) classed as Professionals; generally lower-skilled workers (laborers, housekeepers, mill workers, etc.) classed as Laborers; all others (housewives, unemployed, etc.) as Others.

7. Data on patient statistics was compiled by the author from the *Annual Reports of Sisters of Charity Hospital, Saint Mary's General Hospital, 1893–1908, 1910,* SOCSHA. Full reports for the years 1897 and 1898 have not been preserved. The entire 1909 report has been lost. The 1910 report contains a summation of data for the hospital since its beginning in 1893, which contains data for the year 1909. SOCSHA.

8. See Table 4, Appendix B.

9. Data on patient statistics was complied by the author from the *Annual Reports for Central Maine General Hospital, 1893–1908.* The Central Maine General Hospital fiscal year was originally from July 1st to June 30th. In 1894, this was changed to October 1st to September 30th. The reports for fiscal year 1894 included data from July 1, 1893 to September 30, 1894. CMMC.

10. Only 48 cases reported between 1893–1908. See Table 4, Appendix C.

11. See Table 4, Appendix B and Table 4, Appendix C.

12. See notes 7 and 9 above.

13. See Tables 4 and 5, Appendix B (23 deaths and 405 cases) and Tables 4 and 5, Appendix C (10 deaths and 48 cases).

14. *Ibid.*

15. *Ibid.*

16. Calculated by the author from the data compiled from the various annual reports as 2.39 for Sainte-Marie and 0.77 for central Maine. See notes 7 and 9 above.

17. See note 7 above.

18. See note 9 above.

19. See Table 2, Appendix C.

20. *Fourteenth Annual Report of the Directors of the Central Maine General Hospital,* 13, CMMC.

21. *Fifteenth Annual Report of the Directors of the Central Maine General Hospital,* 16, CMMC.

22. *Fourteenth Annual Report of the Directors of the Central Maine General Hospital,* 7, CMMC.

23. See Table 2, Appendix B.

NOTES TO CHAPTER NINE

1. *Eighth Annual Report of the Receipts and Expenditures of the City of Lewiston for the Fiscal year Ending February 28, 1871*, 8–9.
2. *Ibid.*
3. The 1903–1904, 1908–1909 attendance records from the Saint Pierre School detail the seasonal attendance of French Canadian children as they left the school to work. *Ecole Saint Pierre, 1903–1904, 1908–1909*, in possession of author.
4. "Progress of Catholicism," *The Metropolitan Catholic Almanac* (Baltimore, 1851), 235. Quoted in Kauffman, *Ministry & Meaning*, 65.
5. Laura Offenhartz Greene, *Child labor then and now*, 21.
6. Glazier & Shelley, eds. *The Encyclopedia of American Catholic History*, 75.
7. Chronique, 13, SOCSHA.
8. Drawer, "Lewiston Parishes," File, "Saint Peter and Paul," PCA; Box Saint Peter and Paul, FAHC.
9. Files, "Education, Lewiston," PCA.
10. Chronique No. 2, SOCSHA. Drawer 1, File 1, SPPA.
11. When the Grey Nuns were required to perform a teaching ministry their primary focus was the education of young women. It must be emphasized; however, that teaching was and is not the primary vocation of the Grey Nuns. Interview, Sister Jacqueline Peloquin. October 24, 2002.
12. Chronique, No. 2, SOCSHA.
13. Journal, 1884–1894, SOCHA.
14. Chronique, No. 2 dated the founding of the Dames of Charity as either January or February 1879. This lay organization was attached to the parish of Saint Peter and Paul that supported their founding in the 1870s, SOCSHA.
15. File, "Dames de Charité," 2, SPPA.
16. Journal 1884–1894, SOCHA.
17. *Procès verbaux des visites de la Supérieure Générale 'a l Hôpital de la Charité, Lewiston Maine, du 5 janvier 1883 au 6 mars 1979*, trans. Peloquin and Hudson, SOCSHA.
18. *Historic Lewiston A Textile City in Transition*, Produced for the Lewiston Historical Commission in Central Maine Vocational Technical Institution, (Auburn, 1976).
19. *Eighth Annual Report City of Lewiston*, 9.
20. It is unclear in the ledgers if this rate was per day, per week, or per finish piece. Payroll Ledger Two Weeks, Ending January 1906, 5. This collection is archived at Lewiston Public Library, LPL.
21. Yves Frenette, quoted in, "To Make a Living: Franco-American Work Traditions in Lewiston and Auburn" *Lewiston-Auburn College* (April 24–May 31, 1994), 3.

22. Vicero, "Immigration of French Canadians to New England," 322, 328.

23. Edwin M. Snow, *Report Upon the Census of Rhode Island, 1875,CXX* Quoted in Vicero, "Immigration of French Canadians to New England," 329.

24. Chronique, SOCSHA.

25. Sommaire, 3, SOCHA.

26. *Annual Report of the Girl's Orphanage of Lewiston, Maine Under the Auspices of the Sisters of Charity, 1908,* 6, SOCSHA.

27. The Sisters of St. Joseph of Carondelet were also a French order of women religious who came to the United States in 1836. See Coburn and Smith, *Spirited Lives,* 51.

28. The report does not clarify the relationship of the "relative" to the orphan being released to their care. *Annual Report of the Girls' Orphanage of Lewiston, Maine under the Auspices of the Sisters of Charity, 1908,* 7, SOCSHA.

29. The 1880 Registre and the 1885–1904 Sommaire of the Grey Nuns' community in Lewiston are preserved. The data in the Registre and the Sommaire is not systematic, but rather, varies with each writer. To whom the children were released to and where they went after leaving the Grey Nuns' care was not recorded. The conclusion is supported by the Saint-Hyacinthe Archivist, Sister Marie-Paule Messier, 2001. SOCSHA.

30. There is no account in the annual reports that show what percentage of orphans had lost either one or both parents. *Annual Report of the Girls Orphanage,* 15. SOCSHA.

31. *Registre 1 & 2, 1880–1906.* SOCHA.

32. *Ibid.*

33. Registry Deed, Book 75, Page 280, No. 778, October 5, 1881, Androscoggin Country Registry of Deeds, ACCH.

34. *Annual Report, Healy Asylum, 1896,* 1, SOCSHA.

35. *Ibid,* 3–4. SOCSHA.

36. *Ibid,* 2–3. SOCSHA.

37. *Ibid,* 2. SOCSHA.

38. Letter dated March 20, 1900. PCA

39. *Ibid.*

40. Dion letter dated March 30, 1900, PCA.

41. *Ibid.*

42. Letter dated July 9, 1900, PCA. Due to the penmanship of Sister Dion the correct spelling of the name of the child identified as Johnnie Britting is problematic.

43. Letter dated November 23, 1900, PCA.

44. Letter dated June 27, 1901, PCA.

45. Letter dated June 12, 1901, PCA.

46. See Michael J. Guignard, "The Corporate Sole Controversy," *Steeples and Smokestacks,* Claire Quintal, ed. 198–200. An excellent anthology of the theological responses to specific social tensions in the American Church is Patrick W. Carey ed. *American Catholic Religious Thought.*

47. Maria Harris, *Dance of the Spirit*, 40.

NOTES TO THE CONCLUSION

1. Brown and McKeown, *The Poor Belong to us*, 3.
2. Foucault, *The History of Sexuality*, 87.
3. Sommaire 1885–1904, 21, SOCHA.
4. Chroniques, SOCSHA. Also see, Drawer, "Bishop Healy," File, "Healy Papers," PCA.
5. Chroniques, SOCSHA.

NOTES TO APPENDIX A

1. File: Lewiston, Saint Patrick's Parish Records, 1874, PCA.
2. Blank cells are due to missing/destroyed or otherwise unavailable records.
3. Data for Saint Joseph parish is held in the Saint Patrick file, see Box: Parish Records, 1874, File Lewiston, Saint Patrick's, PCA; Saint Joseph Rectory, Parish Records, Lewiston, Maine.
4. Saint Patrick's Parish, Box: Parish records, 1879, File Saint Patrick's Lewiston, PCA.

NOTES TO APPENDIX B

1. Data on patient statistics was compiled by the author from the *Annual Reports of Sisters of Charity Hospital, Saint Mary's General Hospital, 1893–1908, 1910*, SOCSHA. Full reports for the years 1897 and 1898 have not been preserved.
2. The 1909 Annual Report was not preserved. The 1910 Annual Report was preserved and it contains a summation for the hospital beginning in 1893 which contains data for the year 1909. SOCSHA.
3. This information was irregularly characterized and reported by both hospitals in their annual reports. For comparative purposes, four consecutive years for each hospital were selected for calculation of percentages of occupations; since this data was not reported for all years, this meant that different four year periods were selected for each hospital. The occupation categories were developed by the author in the following manner: skilled craftsmen (carpenters, masons, painters, printers, shoemakers, etc.) classed as Artisans; office and formally educated workers (managers, clerks, doctors, nurses, ship captains, etc.) classed as Professionals; generally lower-skilled workers (laborers, housekeepers, mill workers, etc.) classed as Laborers; all others (housewives, unemployed, etc.) as Others.
4. This table represents the conditions diagnosed for patients reporting to, and treated by, the medical department of the hospital. It does not address the patients seen in the walk-in clinics or the surgical department. With the development of contemporary diagnostic skills medical terminology

has changed. Thus some groupings of medical conditions were done to construct a more inclusive category.

5. The "Other" category was unspecified in the original reports.

NOTES TO APPENDIX C

1. Data for this appendix is taken from the *Annual Reports for Central Maine General Hospital, 1893-1908*. The Central Maine General Hospital fiscal year was originally from July 1st to June 30th. In 1894, this was changed to October 1st to September 30th. The reports for fiscal year 1894 included data from July 1, 1893 to September 30, 1894. CMMC.

2. After 1903, Central Maine General Hospital did not report the actual number of subsidized patients. The numbers provided in this table for 1904-1906 are estimates determined by the number of weeks recorded of both "free" and "paid" care and dividing those weeks by reported average patient length of stay for those years. Central Maine General Hospital did not provide any information about subsidized patients in its reports for 1907 to 1910.

3. See endnote 3, Appendix B. Results for "Others" strongly influenced by Central Maine General Hospital's occupation classes of "Housewife" and "None," Hospital General Sainte-Marie did not report such categories as occupations.

4. Determined using the same methods as for the Hospital General Sainte-Marie data reported in Appendix B, Table 4.

5. "Other" category was unspecified in original reports.

NOTES TO APPENDIX D

1. Claude-Marie Gagnon, *La Maison Jaune*, 267–344, SOCSHA; *Soeurs de la Mission, Hospital General Sainte-Marie, SOCSHA; Liste Générale des Soeurs de la Charité de Saint-Hyacinthe, Février 1977*, SOCSHA; Correspondence, Sister Marie-Paule Messier, Archivist, November 9, 1999. Information provided per the permission of the Sister of Charity, Montreal, Canada, October 2005.

2. Interview with Marie-Paule Messier, Archivist, November 7, 2000; "Liste Générale des Soeurs de la Charité de Saint-Hyacinthe" (Février 1977), 8. SOCSHA.

3. Correspondence with Congregation Archivist, Sister Marie-Paule Messier, December 15, 1999.

4. Albina Archambault had a distinguish career at Saint Mary's General Hospital beyond the conclusion of this study. In 1923 she was the Lewiston Superior. SOCSHA.

5. Georgienne Jacques died prior to making her final profession. SOCSHA.

6. Eléonore Paquette was a Franco-American born in Newton, New Hampshire. She would return to Saint Mary's General Hospital in 1919. She worked again as a pharmacist until her departure in 1931. SOCSHA.

7. Alphonsine Drapeau did not leave Saint Mary's General Hospital until 1918. From 1913-1918 she worked in the convent's refectory. SOCSHA.
8. Arzelie Guertin was a sister-nurse on the wards from 1910-1916. She then retuned in 1922 and worked in the operating room. SOCSHA.
9. Aurelie Biron was a petit sister. It is unclear if her involvement with Saint Mary's General Hospital was uninterrupted from 1899-1932. In 1900 she is credited with working on the geriatric wards, and bathrooms; 1916 the sacristy; 1918 the sacristy; 1932 bathrooms and sacristy. SOCSHA.
10. Marie-Anna Millette would return to work at Saint Mary's General Hospital in 1919. SOCSHA.

Bibliography

NOTE ON SOURCES

The primary material on the Grey Nuns, Hospital General Sainte-Marie, the Girls' Orphanage, and the Healy Asylum is held at the Grey Nuns' archive in Saint-Hyacinthe and at Saint Mary's Regional Medical Center, Lewiston, Maine. These repositories contain data on individual sisters, organization of the order, hospital accounts, orphans, illness and ethnicity of patients. Access to material pertaining to individual sisters is limited due to legal and the community's own rule of privacy. Furthermore a Grey Nun seldom signed her own work or brought attention to her endeavors and accomplishments. Nevertheless, the annuals, chronicles, and Superior General Reports were a rich source that provided the essential historical criticism required in this work.

Available in the Portland Chancery diocesan archive is a partial collection of letters and correspondence between the Catholic hierarchy and the Grey Nuns. The yearly summary of the parish accounts for Saint Pierre/Saint Peter and Paul, Saint Joseph, and Saint Patrick are also held at this archive; as well as material pertaining to the lives of the Portland Bishops Bacon, Healy, Walsh and O'Connell. A collection on Saint Mary's Regional Medical Center by the diocesan archivist was not begun until 1940. Source material from physicians who worked with the Grey Nuns and in their hospital has not been consistently preserved in any known archive.

All source material on the Grey Nuns was made available to me at the discretion of the community's archivist Sister Marie-Paul Messier, the then Portland Superior Sister Jacqueline Peloquin and the Superior General. I remain forever honored by their openness to my research and trust. It was a privilege to work with the Grey Nuns of Saint-Hyacinthe, Quebec.

LIST OF ABBREVIATIONS

ACCH   Androscoggin County Court House, Auburn, Maine

ACHS   Androscoggin County Historical Society, Auburn, Maine

ACMA   Androscoggin County Medical Association

CMGH   Central Maine General Hospital

CMMC   Central Maine Medical Center

FAHC   Franco-American Heritage Collection, University of Maine, Lewiston-Auburn Campus, Lewiston, Maine

LPL   Lewiston, Public Library, Lewiston, Maine

LWPC   Lewiston Water Power Company

MSL   Maine State Library, Augusta, Maine

PCA   Portland Chancery Archives, Portland, Maine

SMGH   Saint Mary's General Hospital (renamed Saint Mary's Regional Medical Center)

SOCHA   Sisters of Charity Hospital Archives, Saint Mary's Regional Medical Center, Lewiston, Maine

SOCSHA   Sisters of Charity Saint-Hyacinthe Archives, Saint-Hyacinthe, Quebec

SPPA   Saints Peter and Paul Archives

PRIMARY SOURCES

Archives

American-Canadian Genealogical Society, Father Leo E. Begin Chapter, Lewiston, Maine:

> *Necrology of Saint Peter and Paul Cemetery.*

Central Maine Medical Center, Lewiston, Maine:

> *Annual Reports,* Central Maine General Hospital, Lewiston, Maine, for the years 1892–1910.
> Notes, pictures, and written accounts on the founding of Central Maine General Hospital.

Chancery of the Diocese of Portland, Portland, Maine:

> Bishop Healy's *Diary*
> *History of Parishes, Book II, East Millinocket thru Lubec*
> Box: *Parish Records 1874*

Drawers of correspondence, writings, reports, and other materials related to the following and organized alphabetically:

> Auburn-Saint Lewis
> Bishop Bacon
> Bishop Healy
> Bishop Walsh
> Lewiston-Saint Patrick and Saint Peter and Paul
> Lewiston-Holy Family, Saint Mary, Saint Joseph
> Women Religious

Binder labeled Clergy D-K:

> Personal information and histories on members on clergy.

Binder labeled Parish Histories.
> Materials relating to the history of Catholicism in Maine.

Congregation of Notre Dame de Sion (Sisters of Sion) Saskatoon, Saskatchewan, Canada:

> Materials on personal history of congregation members.

Congregation of Saint Dominic of Nancy, the Dominican Sisters, Sabattus, Maine:

> Materials on personal history of congregation members and early history of the congregation.

Congregation of the Sisters of Charity of Montreal, Grey Nuns, Guy Street, Montreal:

> Materials on Saint Marguerite D'Youville.
> Material on personal history of congregation members.
> Oral histories of individual Grey Nuns, memorialized in author's personal notes.
> Collection of articles written by various congregation members.

Congregation of the Sisters of Charity of Saint-Hyacinthe, Quebec, Canada:

> *Annales des Soeurs de la Charité de Saint-Hyacinthe,* for the years 1878 to 1908
> *Annual Reports,* Saint Mary's General Hospital, Lewiston, Maine for the years 1892–1908, 1910.
> *Chroniques des Soeurs de la Charité de Saint-Hyacinthe* for the years 1840–1908.
> *Constitutions,* 1840, 1970.
> Gagnon, Claude-Marie *La Maison Jaune: Les Soeurs de la Charité de Saint-Hyacinthe.* Quebec: Fides, 1990.
> Materials related to the founding of the congregation, hospital, orphanages, and schools of nursing.
> Materials on the personal history of congregation members.
> *Visites de La Supérieure Générale,* 1883–1909.

Congregation of the Sisters of Providence, of Saint Mary-of-the-Woods, Indiana:

> Letters by Bishop Celestine de la Hailandiere to Mother Theodore Guerin, 1841.
>
> Materials on personal history of congregation members.

Congregation of the Sisters of Providence, Seattle, Washington:

> Letters of Mother Joseph of the Sacred Heart.
>
> Material related to the founding of hospitals in the Pacific Northwest.

Congregation of the Ursuline Sisters, Ursuline Monastery, Quebec, Canada:

> Material related to Sister Mary of the Incarnation.

Franco-American Heritage Collection, University of Maine, Lewiston-Auburn Campus, Lewiston, Maine:

> Photograph Collection.
>
> Materials on Saint Mary's General Hospital.
>
> Materials on Lewiston's French Canadian community.

Lewiston Armory, Lewiston, Maine

> The Libby Mill Collection (material in storage for archiving)

Lewiston Public Library, Lewiston, Maine

> The Franklin Company Collection
>
> The Lewiston Room Collection.

McGill University, Montreal, Quebec, Canada:

> Peter Gossage. "Abandoned Children in Nineteenth Century Montreal." MA Thesis, McGill University (September 1983).

Saint Mary's Regional Medical Center, Lewiston, Maine:

> *Registres 1* and *2,*1880–1906.
>
> *Journal,* 1884–1894.
>
> *Sommaires,* 1885–1904, 1904–1914.
>
> Photographs.
>
> Materials from the Office of Mission Effectiveness related to the Grey Nuns.

Interviews

Sister Solange Bernier, OSU. Lewiston, Maine (September 21, 1998).

Sister Céline, OP. Sabattus, Maine (September 8, 1998).

Sister Marie-Paule Messier, SOCSH, Congregation's Archivist, Saint-Hyacinthe, Quebec (November 7–8, 2000).

Cathy Montego, Lewiston, Maine (August 22, 2002).

Sister Jacqueline Peloquin, SOCSH, Portland Superior, Portland, Maine April 16, 2001, October 30, 2001, October 24, 2002, October 5, 2005.

Julie Waite, Assistant, Temple Shalom, Auburn, Maine (March 19, 2003).

Census Records, Directories and Almanacs, Newspapers

Federal Census and Governmental Records

Validation Books, City of Lewiston, for the years 1881, 1883, 1884, 1885, 1886, 1887, 1888, 1889, and 1890.
Massachusetts, Bureau of Statistics of Labor, *Thirteenth Annual Report,* 1882.
Tenth Census of the United States, Volume I, 1880.
Eleventh Census of the United States 1890.

Directories, Almanacs, and Encyclopedias

C.T. Onions, ed. *Oxford Universal Dictionary on Historical Principles.* Oxford: Oxford University Press, 1933.
Catechism of the Catholic Church, Libreria Editrice Vaticana, English Translation, United States Catholic Conference, Inc. 1994.
Encyclopedia of American Catholic History, Michael Glazier and Thomas J. Shelley, editors. New York: The Liturgical Press, 1997.
Encyclopedia of World History, New York: George Philip Limited, 2000.
First Annual Report on Birth, Marriages, Divorces & Deaths, in the State of Maine, Year ending December 31, 1892. August: Burleigh & Flynt, 1894.
Greenought & Company, Directory of the Inhabitants, Institutions, Manufacturing Establishment, Business, Societies, Business Firms, Etc., Etc., In The Cities of Lewiston & Auburn. Boston: Greenought & Company, 1874–1910.
New Catholic Encyclopedia. New York: McGraw-Hill Books, 1967.
Official Catholic Directories and *Almanacs,* 1864–1910.
Sadlier's Catholic Directory, Almanac, and Ordo for the Year of Our Lord, 1880 (New York: D & J Sadlier and Company, 1880).
Stedman's Medical Dictionary 27th Edition. Philadelphia: Lippincott, Williams & Wilkins, 2000.

Newspapers

Le Messager (Lewiston, Maine).
Lewiston Sun Journal.
Lewiston Morning.
Le Courrier de Saint-Hyacinthe (Saint-Hyacinthe, Quebec).

Articles and Reports

Giguere, Madeleine. "Remarks for Jan Hitchcock's Culture, Behavior and Personality." Lewiston-Auburn College. (October 1994).
———. To Make a Living: Franco-American Work Traditions in Lewiston and Auburn." Atrium Gallery, Lewiston-Auburn College University of Southern Maine. (April 24-May 31, 1994).
Giguere, Madeleine and Carmel Laverdiere, "Chronology SS. Peter and Paul Parish, 1870–1996, Lewiston, Maine," Diocese of Portland (September–June, 1995–1996).

Loyal Orange Institution. *Annual Report and Proceeding of the Grand Lodge of Maine, Eighteenth Annual Session.* Bangor, Maine (March 1913).

Parker, Peter J. "History of the Franklin Company and related Enterprises." *The Franklin Company and Related Enterprises: A Guide to their Records in the Lewiston Public Library."* Prepared by Christopher Beam. (February 1997).

Toner, J. M. "Statistics of Regular Medical Associations and Hospitals of the United States," *Transaction of the American Medical Association* 24 (1873): 314–333.

The Social Settlement of Lewiston and Auburn (Maine) Incorporated 1900, Oxford Court, Corner Lincoln and Cedar Sts. Year Book 1902.

Books

Alcott, Louisa May. *Hospital Sketches: An Army Nurse's True Account of her Experience During the Civil War.* 1863; reprint, Bedford: Applewood Books, 1993.

Ferland-Angers, Albertine. *Mother D'Youville: First Canadian Foundress.* Translation by Richard R. Cooper. Montreal: Sisters of Charity of Montreal, "Grey Nuns," 2000.

En Feuilletant les Chroniques de L'Hôtel-Dieu de S.-Hyacinthe et des Maisons Qui En Dependent. Saint-Hyacinthe: Société D'Histoire Régionale, 1940.

"Maria Monk." *Awful Disclosures of the Hotel Dieu Nunnery.* Hamden, Connecticut: Archon Books, 1962 Reprint New York: Howe and Bates, 1836.

Mother Theodore Guerin, Journals and Letters. Indiana: Saint Mary-of-the-Woods, 1937.

Travels of Mother Frances Xavier Cabrini: Foundress of the Missionary Sisters of the Sacred Heart of Jesus. Milwaukee: The Missionary Sisters of the Sacred Heart of Jesus, 1944.

SECONDARY SOURCES

Dissertations, Papers and Publications

Allen, James Paul. "Catholics in Maine: A Social Geography." Ph.D. dissertation, Syracuse University, 1970.

Badeau, Marie Paul. *A Rich Past—A Challenging Future, A Tribute to SS. Peter and Paul Parish, Paroisse St. Pierre et St. Paul.* (Lewiston: Penmor Lithographers, 1996).

Burgess, J.H., ed. "Franco-Americans of the State of Maine U.S.A. and Their Achievements: Historical, Descriptive and Biographical." Compiled by R.J. Lawton. Lewiston: H.F. Roy, 1915.

Cummings, Kathleen Sprows. "Change of Habit." *American Catholic Studies Newsletter,* Cushwa Center for the Study of American Catholicism. 29 (Spring 2002): 1, 8–11.

Hodgkin, Douglas I. "Managing the Poor in Lewiston, Maine, 1795–1863." Presented at *Washburn Humanities Conference: Northern New England in the Nineteenth Century.* Norlands, Livermore, Maine, June 2001.

Hudson, Susan Pearman. "God Deliver Me From Gloomy Saints." MA Thesis, University of Portland, 1992.

———. "Les Soeurs Grises of Lewiston Maine, 1878–1910: An ethnic Religious Feminist Expression." Working paper, presented to National Association for Women in Catholic Higher Education, Boston College, Massachusetts, June 30, 2000.

———. "Les Soeurs Grises of Lewiston, Maine, 1878–1910: An Ethnic Religious Feminist Expression." Presented at *History of Women Religious* Conference, Marquette University, Milwaukee, June 18, 2001.

———. "Medicine for the Masses: The Social Dynamics of Lewiston's Hospitals, 1888–1910." Presented at *Washburn Humanities Conference New England in the Nineteenth Century*, Norlands, Livermore, Maine, June 3, 2000.

———. "Spirituality in the History of Care: The Grey Nuns of Lewiston, Maine." Presented at *Washburn Humanities Conference New England in the Nineteenth Century*, Norlands, Livermore, Maine, June 9, 2001.

———. "The World of French-Canadian Women in Lewiston, Maine: Issues of Rights and Rites." Presented at *Washburn Humanities Conference New England in the Nineteenth Century*, Norlands, Livermore, Maine, June 12, 1999.

———. "Lewiston's Franco-American Women." Presented at *Muskie Millennial Series*, Bates College, Lewiston Maine, October 14, 1999.

Kuss, Kurt F. "That's Freewill, Not Freewheelin:' An Introduction to Freewill Baptists, 1780 to 1868." Presented at *Washburn Humanities Conference New England in the Nineteenth Century*, Norlands, Livermore, Maine, June 9, 2001.

Marguerite d'Youville: Great Moments in Canadian Church History, Canada, (Circa 1980).

Myhrman, A. M., Rademaker, J.A. "The Second Colonization Process in an Industrial Community" Typescript. Lewiston Public Library. Circa 1943.

Richard, Mark Paul. "Out of 'Little Canada:' The Assimilation of Sainte-Famille Parish, Lewiston, Maine, 1923–1994." M.A. Thesis, University of Maine, August 1994.

Shannon, Christopher. "Towards a History of Suffering," *American Catholic Studies Newsletter*, Cushwa Center for the Study of American Catholicism. 27 (Fall 2000): 1, 7–10.

Thompson, Margaret Susan. "To Serve the People of God; Nineteenth-Century Sisters and the Creation of an American Religious Life." *Working Paper Series* 18, 2. Notre Dame, Indiana: Charles and Margaret Hall Cushwa Center for the Study of American Catholicism, 1987.

Vicero, Ralph Dominic. "Immigration of French Canadians to New England, 1840–1900: A Geographical Analysis." Ph.D. dissertation, University of Wisconsin, 1968.

Wall, Barbra Mann. "Unlikely Entrepreneurs: Nuns, Nursing, and Hospital Development in the West and Midwest, 1865–1915." Ph.D. dissertation, Notre Dame, 2000.

Winthrop, Reverend Katharine Hope. "Give Them Not Hell, But Hope and Courage." Presented at *Washburn Humanities Conference New England in the Nineteenth Century*, Norlands, Livermore, Maine, June 9, 2002.

Wittberg, Patricia SC. "Back to the Future: The Current Paradigm Shift in Women's Religious Communities." Presented at *History of Women Religious* Conference, Marquette University, Milwaukee, June 19, 2001.

Articles and Works in Anthologies

Allen, James P. "The Franco-Americans in Maine: A Geographical Perspective." In *A Franco-American Overview, Volume 3*. ed. Madeleine Giguere. Cambridge, Massachusetts, National Assessment and Dissemination Center, 1981.

Amundsen, Darrel W. "Medicine and Faith in Early Christianity," *Bulletin of the History of Medicine* 56 (1982): 326–350.

Clevenger, Sydney. "St. Vincent's and the Sisters of Providence: Oregon's First Permanent Hospital." *Oregon Historical Quarterly* 102 (Summer 2001): 210–221.

Donohue, John W. "Sisters in Mercy, Florence Nightingale and Mother Mary Clare More." *America* 184 (June 4–11, 2001): 14–19.

Doorley, Michael. "Irish Catholics and French Creoles: Ethnic Struggles within the Catholic Church in New Orleans." *The Catholic Historical Review* 75 (January 2001): 34–54.

Dossey, Barbara M. and Larry Dossey. "Attending to Holistic Care: It's Time We Listened to our Patients' Concerns about Soul and Spirit." *American Journal of Nursing* 98 (August 1998): 35–37.

Doyle, Ann. "Nursing by Religious Orders in the United States, Part II—1841–1870." *American Journal of Nursing* 29 (August 1929): 959–969.

Drachman, Virginia G. "The Loomis Trial: Social Mores and Obstetrics in the Mid-Nineteenth Century." In *Health Care in America: Essays in Social History,* edited by Susan Reverby and David Rosner. Philadelphia: Temple University Press, 1979.

Frenette, Yves. "Understanding the French Canadians of Lewiston, 1860–1900: An Alternative Framework." *Maine Historical Society Quarterly* 25 (Spring 1986): 198–229.

Getz, Lorine M. "Women Struggle for an American Catholic Identity." In *Women and Religion in America, Volume 3: 1900–1968*, ed. Rosemary Radford Ruether and Rosemary Skinner Keller. San Francisco: Harper & Row, Publishers, 1986.

Goode, William J. "Community Within a Community: The Professions." *American Sociological Review* 22 (April, 1957): 194–200.

Greeley, Andrew. "The Revolutionary Events of Vatican II: How Everything Changed. *Commonweal* 125 (September 11, 1998): 15.

Guignard, Michael. "The Case of the Sacred Heart Parish." *Maine Historical Society Quarterly* 22 (Summer 1982): 21–36.

———. "The Corporation Sole Controversy." In *Steeples and Smokestacks;* ed. Claire Quintal. Worcester: Institut français Assumption College, 1996.

———. "The Corporation Sole Controversy." *Maine Historical Society,* Newsletter 12 (September 11, 1998): 15.

Klandermans, Bert. "Mobilization and Participation: Social-Psychological Expansions of Resource Mobilization Theory." *American Sociological Review* 49 (October 1984): 583–600.

Leamon, James S. *Historical Lewiston: A Textile City in Transition*. Auburn: Lewiston Historical Commission, 1976: 27–47.

Leamon, James S. and Grinley Barrows. "Little Canada and Vicinity." *Historical Lewiston Franco-American Origins* (Auburn, 1964): 21–36.

Mitchell, Terri. "The Sisters of Providence Archives, Seattle." *Oregon Historical Quarterly* 102 (Summer 2001): 222–228.

Oates, Mary J. "Organized Voluntarism: The Catholic Sisters in Massachusetts, 1870–1940." In *Women in American Religion*, ed. Janet Wilson James. Philadelphia: University of Pennsylvania Press, 1978.

Piotrowski, Thaddeus M. "The Franco-American Heritage in Manchester, New Hampshire." In *A Franco-American Overview, Volume I*. Compiled by Renaud S. Albert. Cambridge, Massachusetts: National Assessment and Dissemination Center, 1979.

Podea, Iris Saunders. "Quebec to Little Canada: The Coming of the French-Canadians to New England in the Nineteenth Century." In *A Franco-American Overview, Volume 3: New England Part One*, ed. Madeleine Giguere. Cambridge, Massachusetts: National Assessment and Dissemination Center, 1981.

Reiss, Albert J. Jr. "Occupational Mobility of Professional Workers," *American Sociological Review* 20 (December 1955): 693–700.

Richard, Mark Paul. "Coping before L'Etat-providence: Collective Welfare Strategies of New England's Franco-Americans." *Quebec Studies* 25 (Spring 1998): 59–61.

Roby, Yves. "A Portrait of the Female Franco-American Worker (1865–1930)." In *Steeples and Smokestacks* ed. Claire Quintal. Worcester: Institut français Assumption College, 1996: 544–563.

Rosenberg, Charles E. "And Heal the Sick: The Hospital and the Patient in the 19th Century American." *Journal of Social History* 10 (Summer 1977): 428–447.

———. "The Origins of the American Hospital System." *Bulletin of New York Academy of Medicine* 55 (January 1979): 10–21.

———. "Social Class and Medical Care in Nineteenth-Century America: The Rise and Fall of the Dispensary." *Journal of the History of Medicine* 29 (January 1974): 32–54.

———. "The Therapeutic Revolution: Medicine, Meaning, and Social Change in Nineteenth-Century America." *Perspective in Biology and Medicine* (Summer 1977): 485–506.

Sewell, William H. Jr. "A Theory of Structure: Duality, Agency, and Transformation," *American Journal of Sociology* 98 (July 1992): 1–29.

Sklar, Kathryn Kish. "The Historical Foundation of Women's Power in the Creation of the American Welfare States." In *Mothers of a New World: Maternalist Politics and the Origins of Welfare State*. eds. Seth Koven and Sonya Mitchel. New York: Routledge, Inc. 1993; 43–93.

Spaulding, Thomas W., CFX. "The Catholic Frontiers." *U.S. Catholic Historian* 12 (Fall 1994): 1–15.

Taves, Ann. "Women and Gender in American Religion(s)." *Religious Studies Review* 18 (October 1992): 263–269.

Tentler, Leslie Woodcock. "On the Margins: The State of American Catholic History." *American Quarterly* 45 (March 1993): 104–27.

Thompson, Margaret Susan. "Sisterhood and Power: Class, Culture, and Ethnicity in the American Convent." *Colby Library Quarterly* 25 (1989): 149–75.

Vicero, Ralph. "Sources statistiques pour l'étude de l'immigration et du peuplement Canadien-Francais en Nouvelle-Angleterre au cours XIXe siècle." *Initiating Franco-American Studies* eds. Stanley L. Freeman, Jr., and Raymond J. Pelletier (Orono: University of Maine, 1981).

Vogel, Morris J. "The Transformation of the American Hospital, 1850–1920." In *Health Care in America*. eds. Susan Reverby & David Rosner. (Philadelphia: Temple University Press, 1979): 105–117.

Wade, Mason. "French and French-Canadians in the United States." In *A Franco-American Overview, Volume 3,* edited by Madeleine Giguere. Cambridge, Massachusetts National Assessment and Dissemination Center, 1981.

———. "French and French Canadians in the U.S." In *New Catholic Encyclopedia* 6. New York: McGraw-Hill Books, 1967.

———. "The French Parish and "Survivance" in 19th Century New England." In *A Franco-American Overview, Volume 3,* edited by Madeleine Giguere. Cambridge, Massachusetts, National Assessment and Dissemination Center, 1981.

Wall, Barbra Mann. "We Might as Well Burn It': Catholic Sister-Nurses and Hospital Control, 1865–1930." *Catholic Historian* 20 (Winter 2002): 21–39.

Widerquist, Joann G. "The Spirituality of Florence Nightingale." *Nursing Research* 41 (1992): 49–55.

Woodbury, Kenneth B Jr. "An Incident Between the French Canadians and the Irish in the Diocese of Maine in 1906." *The New England Quarterly* 45 (June 1976): 60–269.

Books

Abramson, Harold J. *Ethnic Diversity in Catholic America.* New York, London, Sydney, Toronto: John Wiley & Sons, 1973.

Addams, Jane. *Twenty Years at Hull-House with Autobiographical Notes.* 1910; reprint, Urbana and Chicago: University of Illinois Press, 1990.

Alvord, Lori Arviso, and Elizabeth Cohen Van Pelt. *The Scalpel and the Silver Bear: The First Navajo Woman Surgeon Combines Western Medicine and Traditional Healing.* New York, Toronto, London, Sydney, Auckland: Bantam Books, 1999.

Anderson, Bonnie S. and Judith P. Zinsser. *A History of Their Own, Volume One.* New York: Harper & Row Publishers, 1988.

Appleby, R. Scott. *"Church and Age Unite!:" The Modernist Impulse in American Catholicism.* Notre Dame, Indiana: University of Notre Dame Press, 1993.

Ashly, JoAnn. *Hospitals, Paternalism and the Role of the Nurse.* (New York: Teachers College Press, 1976).

Bokenkotter, Thomas. *A Concise History of the Catholic Church.* New York: Image Books, Doubleday, 1990.

Breisach, Ernst A. *American Progressive History, An Experiment in Modernization.* Chicago and London: University of Chicago Press, 1993.

Brewer, Eileen Mary. *Nuns and the education of American Catholic women, 1860–1920.* Chicago: Loyola University Press, 1987.

Brown, Dorothy M., and Elizabeth McKeown. *The Poor belong to us: Catholic Charities and American Welfare*. Cambridge, Massachusetts, and London, England: Harvard University Press, 1997.

Brown, Peter. *The Body and Society: Men, Women, and Sexual Renunciation in Early Christianity*. New York: Columbia University Press, 1988.

Brown, Sister Mary Borromeo. *History of the Sisters of Providence of Saint Mary-Of-The-Woods, Volume I*. New York, Boston, Cincinnati, Chicago, San Francisco: Benziger Brothers, Inc. 1949.

Carey, Patrick W. *People, Priests, and Prelates: Ecclesiastical Democracy and the Tensions of Trusteeism*. Notre Dame, Indiana: University of Notre Dame Press, 1987.

Carey, Patrick W. ed. *American Catholic Religious Thought: The Shaping of a Theological and Social Tradition*. New York/Mahwah: Paulist Press, 1987.

Celeste, Sister Marie, SC. *Elizabeth Ann Seton A Self-Portrait: A Study of Her Spirituality in Her Own Words*. Libertyville: Franciscan Marytown Press, 1986.

Coburn, Carol K. and Martha Smith. *Spirited Lives: How Nuns Shaped Catholic Culture and American Life, 1836–1920*. Chapel Hill and London: University of North Carolina Press, 1999.

Cohen, Lizabeth. *Making a New Deal: Industrial Workers in Chicago, 1919–1939*. Cambridge, New York, Melbourne: Press Syndicate of the University of Cambridge, 1990.

Cott, Nancy F. *The Bonds of Womanhood: "Woman's Sphere" In New England, 1780–1835*. New Haven and London: Yale University Press, 1977.

———. *The Grounding of Modern Feminism*. New Haven and London: Yale University Press, 1987.

Culbertson, Diana, OP. ed. *Rose Hawthorne Lathrop, Selected Writings*. New York and Mahwah: Paulist Press, 1993.

Danylewycz, Marta. *Taking the Veil: An Alternative to Marriage, Motherhood, and Spinsterhood in Quebec, 1840–1920*. Toronto: McClelland and Stewart, 1987.

A Daughter of Saint Paul. *Mother Cabrini*. Boston: Daughters of Saint Paul, 1977.

Dawley, Alan. *Struggles for Justice: Social Responsibility and the Liberal State*. Cambridge, Massachusetts: The Belknap Press of Harvard University Press, 1991.

Demos, John. *The Unredeemed Captive: a Family Story from Early America*. New York: Alfred A. Knopf, 1994.

Diner, Hasia R. *Erin's Daughters in America: Irish Immigrants Women in the Nineteenth Century*. Baltimore: Johns Hopkins University Press, 1983.

Dolan, Jay P. *Catholic Revivalism: The American Experience 1830–1900*. Notre Dame, Indiana and London: University of Notre Dame Press, 1978.

———. *The American Catholic Experience: A History from Colonial Times to the Present*. Notre Dame, Indiana: University of Notre Dame Press, 1992.

———. *The Immigrant Church: New York's Irish and German Catholics 1815–1865*. Notre Dame and London: The University of Notre Dame Press edition, 1983. Originally published Johns Hopkins University Press, 1975.

Donato, Pietro Di. *Immigrant Saint*. New York: McGraw-Hill Book Company, Inc., 1960.

Duchaussois, Rev. Father P., OMI. *The Grey Nuns in the Far North 1867–1917*. Toronto: McClelland and Stewart Ltd. 1919.

Farren, Suzy. *A Call to Care: The Women Who Built Catholic Healthcare In America*. St. Louis, Missouri and Washington D.C.: The Catholic Health Association of the United States, 1996.

Ferland-Angers, Albertine. *Mother D'Youville, First Canadian Foundress*. trans. Richard R. Cooper. Montreal: Sisters of Charity, Montreal, 2000.

Fishman, Joshua A. et al. *Language Loyalty in the United States*. London: Mouton & Co., 1966.

Fitts, Sister Mary Pauline, GNSH. *Hands to the Needy: Marguerite d'Youville Apostle to the Poor, Foundress of the Grey Nuns*. Garden City: Doubleday and Company, Inc., 1987.

Fogarty, Gerald P., SJ. *The Vatican and the American Hierarchy From 1870–1965*. Wilmington, Delaware: Michael Glazier, 1985.

Foley, Albert Sidney, SJ. *Bishop Healy: Beloved Outcast, the Story of a Great Priest whose Life has become a Legend*. New York: Straus and Young, 1954.

Foucault, Michel. *The History of Sexuality, Volume I: An Introduction*. trans. Robert Hurley. New York: Vintage Books, 1980. Original English translation Random House, Inc. 1978.

Gerstle, Gary. *Working-class Americanism: The politics of labor in a textile city, 1914–1960*. Cambridge: Cambridge University Press, 1989.

Giddens, Anthony. *Profiles and Critiques in Social Theory*. Berkeley: University of California Press, 1982.

Giguere, Madeleine, ed. *A Franco-American Overview, Volume 3; New England (Part One)*. Cambridge: National Assessment and Dissemination Center for Bilingual/Bicultural Education, 1981.

Gilbert, James. *Perfect Cities: Chicago's Utopias of 1893*. Chicago and London: University of Chicago Press, 1991.

Ginzburg, Carlo. *The Cheese and The Worms: The Cosmos of a Sixteenth-Century Miller*. trans. John and Anne Tedeschi. Baltimore and London: The John Hopkins University Press, 1980. Originally published in Italy: Giulio Einaudi editore, 1976.

Ginzburg, Lori. *Women and the Work of Benevolence: Morality, Politics, and Class in the Nineteenth-Century United States*. New Haven: Yale University Press, 1990.

Gleason, Philip. *Keeping the Faith: American Catholicism Past and Present*. Notre Dame, Indiana: University of Notre Dame Press, 1987.

Goldfield, David R., Brownell, Blaine A. *Urban America A History, Second Edition*. Boston: Houghton Mifflin Company, 1990.

Gordon, Linda. *The Great Arizona Orphan Abduction*. Cambridge: Harvard University Press, 1999.

Gordon, Linda ed. *Women, the State, and Welfare*. Madison, Wisconsin: University of Wisconsin Press, 1990.

Gossage, Peter. *Families in Transition, Industrial and Population in Nineteenth-Century Saint-Hyacinthe*. Montreal: McGill-Queens University Press, 1999.

Greene Offenhartz, Laura. *Child Labor Then and Now.* New York: Franklin Watts, 1992.

Hale, Robert. *Early Days of Church and State in Maine.* Brunswick: Bowdoin College, 1910.

Hansen, Marcus Lee. *The Mingling of The Canadian and American People, Volume I.* New Haven: Yale University Press; Toronto: The Ryerson Press, 1940.

Hareven, Tamara K. ed. *Family and Kin in Urban Communities, 1700–1930.* New York: New Viewpoints, 1977.

———. "Family time and Industrial time: The relationship between the family and work in a New England industrial community." Cambridge: Cambridge University Press, 1982.

Hareven, Tamara K., and Langerback, Randolph. *Amoskeag: Life and Work in an American Factory City.* New York: Pantheon Books, 1978.

Harris, Maria. *Dance of the Spirit: The Seven Steps of Women's Spirituality.* New York and Toronto: Baton Books, 1989.

Hennessey, James, SJ. *American Catholics: A History Of The Roman Catholic Community In The United States.* New York: Oxford University Press, 1981.

Higgins, Mary Raymond, RSM. *For Love of Mercy: Missioned in Maine and Andros Island, Bahamas, 1883–1983.* Portland, Maine: Sisters of Mercy, 1995.

Hillman, James. *We've Had a Hundred years of Psychotherapy and the World is Getting Worse.* San Francisco: Harper San Francisco, 1992.

House, Adrian. *Francis of Assisi: A Revolutionary Life.* New Jersey: HiddenSpring, 2000.

Howe, Irving. *World of Our Fathers: The Journey of the East European Jews to America and the Life They Found and Made.* New York: Monticello Editions, 1976.

Howell, Joel D. *Technology in the Hospital: Transforming Patient Care in the Early Twentieth Century.* Baltimore and London: John Hopkins University Press, 1995.

Hoy, Suellen. *Chasing Dirt: The American Pursuit of Cleanliness.* New York: Oxford University Press, 1995.

James, Janet Wilson ed. *Women in American Religion.* Philadelphia: University of Pennsylvania Press, 1980.

Kauffman, Christopher J. *Ministry & Meaning: A Religious History of Catholic Health Care in the United States.* New York: Crossroads Publishing Company, 1995.

———. *Faith and Fraternalism: The History of the Knights of Columbus 1882–1982.* New York: Harper and Row Publishers, 1982.

Kaylin, Lucy. *For The Love of God: The Faith and Future of the American Nun.* New York: William Morrow, 2000.

Kenneally, James K. *The History of American Catholic Women.* New York: Crossroad, 1990.

Kennelley, Karen, CSJ, ed. *American Catholic Women: A Historical Explanation.* New York: Basic Books, 1994.

Kerber, Linda K., Alice Kessler-Harris, and Kathryn Kish Sklar. ed. *U.S. History as Women's History: New Feminist Essays.* Chapel Hill and London: University of North Carolina Press, 1995.

Kloppenberg, James T. *Uncertain Victory: Social Democracy and Progressivism in European and American Thought, 1870–1920.* New York and Oxford: Oxford University Press, 1986.

Ladd-Taylor, Molly. *Mother-Work: Women, Child Welfare, and the State, 1890–1930.* Urbana: University of Chicago Press, 1994.

Leamon, James S. *Historical Lewiston: A Textile City in Transition.* Lewiston Historical Commission by Students in the Graphic Arts Department Central Maine Vocational Technical Institute: Auburn, 1976.

Levesque, André. *Making and Breaking the Rules: Women in Quebec, 1919–1939.* trans. Yvonne M. Klein. Toronto: McClelland & Stewart Inc. 1989.

Linteau, Paul-Andre, Rene Durocher, and Jean-Claude Robert. *Quebec A History, 1867–1929.* trans. Robert Chodos. Torondo: James Lorimer & Co. Publishers, 1983.

Liptak, Dolores, RSM. *Heritage of American Catholicism: A Church of Many Cultures.*

———. *Immigrants and Their Church.* New York: MacMillan Publishing Company, 1989.

Lucey, William Leo, SJ. *The Catholic Church in Maine.* Francestown: Marshall Jones Company, 1957.

Maher, Sister Mary Denis. *To Bind Up Their Wounds: Catholic Sister Nurses in the U.S. Civil War.* New York: Greenwood Press, 1989.

Macgregor, Linda Farr. *Rumford Stories.* Rumford: Rumford Public Library, 2000.

Marguerite d'Youville: Foundress of the Grey Nuns. trans. Helena Nantaiz. Montreal: 1949.

Mayer, J.P. ed. *Democracy in America: Alexis de Tocqueville.* trans.George Lawrence, New York: Harper Perennial, 1988, originally published by Harper & Row, 1966.

McDannell, Colleen. *The Christian Home in Victorian America, 1840–1900.* Bloomington: Indiana University Press, 1986.

Michaud, Charlotte, et. al. *Historical Lewiston, Franco-American Origins.* Lewiston: Lewiston Historical Commission, 1974.

Mitchell, Estelle, SGM. *Marguerite d'Youville: Foundress of the Grey Nuns.* trans. Helena Nantais. Montreal: Palm Publishers, 1965.

———. *From the Fatherhood of God to the Brotherhood of Mankind: Marguerite d'Youville's Spiritual Portrait 1701–1771.* trans. Sister Joanna Kerwin. Montreal: Sisters of Charity of Montreal, 1977.

———. *Father Charles Dufrost and his Mother 1729–1790.* trans. Sister Antoinette Bexaire. Montreal: Meridian Press, 1991. English translation Edmonton, Alberta: ABC Press, 1993.

———. *The Spiritual Portrait of Saint Marguerite D'Youville 1701–1771.* trans. Sisters Joanna Kerwin and Antoinette Bexaire GNM. Montreal: Grey Nuns of Montreal, 1993.

Moorhouse, Geoffrey. *Sun Dancing.* San Diego: Harvest Book, 1997.

Morawska, Ewa T. *For bread with butter: The life-worlds of East Central Europeans in Johnstown, Pennsylvania, 1890–1940.* Cambridge and New York: Cambridge University Press, 1985.

Morris, Charles R. *American Catholic: The Saints and Sinners who built Ameri-can's Most Powerful Church.* New York: Vintage Books, 1997.

Muncy, Robyn. *Creating a Female Dominion in American Reform, 1890–1935.* New York: Oxford University Press, 1991.

Nelson, Sioban. *Say Little, Do Much: Nurses, Nuns, and Hospitals in the Nine-teenth Century.* Philadelphia: University of Pennsylvania Press, 2001.

Norris, Kathleen. *The Cloister Walk.* New York: Riverhead Books, 1996.

Nuesse, C.J., Harte, Thomas J., CSsR. *The Sociology of the Parish.* Milwaukee: The Bruce Publishing Co., 1950.

Oates, Mary J. *The Catholic Philanthropic Tradition in America.* Bloomington, Indiana: Indiana University Press, 1995.

O'Brien, David J. *Public Catholicism.* New York: Macmillan, 1989.

Orsi, Robert Anthony. *The Madonna of 115th Street: Faith and Community in Ital-ian Harlem, 1880–1950.* New Haven and London: Yale University Press, 1985.

O'Toole, James M. *Militant and Triumphant: William Henry O'Connell and the Catholic Church in Boston 1859–1944.* Notre Dame and London: University of Notre Dame Press, 1992.

Peiss, Kathy. *Cheap Amusements: Working Women and Leisure in Turn-of-the-Century New York.* Philadelphia: Temple University Press, 1986.

Peterson, William, Michael Novak, and Philip Gleason. *Concepts of Ethnicity.* Cam-bridge, Massachusetts: The Belknap Press of Harvard University Press, 1982.

Philpott, Thomas Lee. *The Slum and the Ghetto: Immigrants, Blacks, and Reform-ers in Chicago, 1880–1930.* 1978: reprint, Belmont: Wadsworth Publishing Company, 1991.

Quintal, Claire, ed. *Steeples and Smokestacks: A Collection of essays on The Franco-American Experience in New England.* Worcester: Institut français Assumption College, 1996.

Remen, Rachel Naomi, MD. *Kitchen Table Wisdom: Stories that Heal.* New York: Riverhead Books, 1994.

Reverby, Susan M. *Ordered to Care: The Dilemma of American Nursing, 1850–1945.* New York: Cambridge University Press, 1987.

Reverby, Susan, and David Rosner, eds. *Health Care In America: Essays in Social History.* Philadelphia: Temple University Press, 1979.

Rioux, Marcel, and Martin, Yves ed. *French Canadian Society, Volume I.* Toronto: McClelland and Steward Limited, 1964.

Roberts, Joan I. and Group, Thetis M. *Feminism and Nursing: An Historical Per-spective on Power, Status, and Political Activism in the Nursing Profession.* Westport, Connecticut and London: Prager, 1995.

Roberts, Jon H. *Darwinism and the Divine in America: Protestant Intellectuals and Organic Evolution 1859–1900.* Madison, Wisconsin: University of Wisconsin Press, 1988.

Roby, Yves. *Les Franco-Américains de la Nouvelle-Angleterre 1776–1930.* Quebec: Septentrion, 1990.

Rosenberg, Charles E. *The Care of Strangers: The Rise of American's Hospital Sys-tem.* New York: Basic Books, Inc., 1987.

Ross, Nancy Wilson. *Westward The Women*. San Francisco: North Point Press, 1985; originally published New York: Random House, 1944.

Ruether, Rosemary Radford, and Keller, Rosemary Skinner ed. *Women and Religion in America, Volume 3: 1900–1968*. San Francisco: Harper & Row, Publishers, 1986.

Rumilly, Robert. *Histoire des Franco-Américains*. Montreal: Edite par L'Auteur, 1958.

Sattin, Antoine, PSS. *Life of Mother d'Youville: Foundress and First Superior of the Sisters of Charity or Grey Nuns*. trans. Georgiana Michaud, SGM. Montreal: Méridien, 1999.

Salzman, Mark. *Lying Awake*. New York: Vintage Books, 2000.

Scott, James C. *Weapons of the Weak: Everyday Forms of Peasant Resistance*. New Haven: Yale University Press, 1985.

Searles, James W. ed. *Immigrants from the North: Franco-Americans Recall the Settlement of their Canadian Families In the Mill Towns of New England."* Bath, Maine: Hyde School, 1982.

Skocpol, Theda. *Protecting Soldiers and Mothers: the Political Origins of Social Policy in the United States*. Cambridge, Massachusetts: Belknap Press of Harvard University Press, 1992.

Smith-Rosenberg, Carroll. *Disorderly Conduct: Visions of Gender in Victorian America*. New York: Alfred a. Knopf, 1985.

Stepsis, Ursula, CSA, and Dolores Liptak, RSM. *Pioneer Healers: The History of Women Religious in American Health Care*. New York: Crossroad Publishing Company, 1989.

Stewart, George C. Jr. *Marvels of Charity: History of American Sisters and Nuns*. Huntington, Indiana: Our Sunday Visitor Publishing Division, 1994.

Taves, Ann. *The Household of Faith: Roman Catholic Devotions in Mid-Nineteenth-Century America*. Notre Dame, Indiana: University of Notre Dame Press, 1986.

Tentler, Leslie Woodcock. *Season of Grace: A History of the Catholic Archdiocese of Detroit*. Detroit: Wayne State University Press, 1990.

Tweed, Thomas A. ed. *Retelling U.S. Religious History*. Berkeley, Los Angeles and London: University of California Press, 1997.

Ulrich, Laurel Thatcher. *Good Wives: Image and Reality in the Lives of Women in Northern New England 1650–1750*. New York: Vintage Books, 1980.

———. *The Life of Martha Ballard, Based on Her Diary 1785–1812*. New York: Alfred A. Knopf, 1990.

An Ursuline of Quebec. *Mary of the Incarnation: Foundress of the Ursuline Monastery*. Ursuline Monastery: Québec, 1939.

Vogel, Morris J. *The Invention of the Modern Hospital: Boston, 1870–1930*. Chicago: University of Chicago Press, 1980.

Wiebe, Robert H. *The Search for Order, 1877–1920*. New York: Hill and Wang, 1967.

Index

For Product Safety Concerns and Information please contact our EU
representative GPSR@taylorandfrancis.com Taylor & Francis Verlag GmbH,
Kaufingerstraße 24, 80331 München, Germany

Printed and bound by CPI Group (UK) Ltd, Croydon, CR0 4YY
08/06/2025
01896982-0003